THIS VAST BEING

THIS VAST BEING

BEING

A Voyage through Grief and Exaltation

By Ann Kreilkamp, Ph.D.
© 2007

LCCN: 2006905115
ISBN-10: 1-934023-20-5
ISBN-13: 978-1-934023-20-4

Lane Schulz, Editor
Jiangmei Wu, Designer
Julia Jackson, Production Manager

Photo credit page 1: Scott Smith
Photo credit insert page 1: Chuck Manners
Photo credit insert page 4: Kate Blackburn

TENDRE PRESS

Tendre Press
134 N. Overhill Dr.
Bloomington, IN 47408
www.tendrepress.com
1-812-337-0192

Contents

To the Reader

I offer this book to you who find yourselves magnetically drawn to death and birth and other significant occasions when the crack between worlds opens and we catch a glimpse of mystery. In the brief hush that follows we sense a larger reality that, if we allow ourselves to open, changes us. Nothing continues as before. The universe fills with meaning.

At this time in western history, we fear mystery, and seem to want to close the crack quickly, to smooth it over and pretend it does not exist. Yet, such crossroads in our lives give us pause—if not in the moment, then they haunt memory.

In the five years prior to my husband's death, I lost a number of people close to me. As each one departed my emotions ricocheted through the usual strong extremes— yet I felt mostly able to fold my grieving process into the routines and obligations of daily life.

Then Jeff died. I look back now on the year that followed and feel intensely grateful for his continued presence, his uncanny wisdom, and his legacy. I hope I have conveyed something of his presence and his wisdom in this book.

His legacy made possible both the book and the experiences that shaped it. As I felt emotionally secure when he was alive, so in death he left me financially secure. This great blessing allowed me to stop my life and consciously immerse myself in the river of remembrance. During that formal mourning process I attempted to bear witness to the currents of my grief, to follow those currents to the sea, to relax my awareness into mystery.

During that year Death reshaped my orientation and joggled loose my preconceived ideas; and Death ignited in me a rush of joy and aliveness so overwhelming that I want to dance and sing to the heavens—
to call the very stars as my witness—
to dive, head first, into the immensity.

Ann Kreilkamp
Bloomington, Indiana

$\mathcal{A}$cknowledgements

Everyone with whom my life intersects benefits me in countless ways. Sometimes I recognize the benefits, usually I do not—or not at the time. Each relationship offers such great blessings, though often hidden within the drama we find ourselves enacting—or re-enacting! The older I grow, the more I recognize the vast wealth that has accrued from over six decades of gathering in Earth's garden with more and more fellow radiant souls.

And yet, to my surprise, during what I like to think of as "my year of conscious grieving," I felt most grateful for the blessings of solitude. So I thank and hug and bless and kiss all my beloveds who, perhaps intuitively sensing my need, left me mostly alone.

Part I

Jackson Hole, Wyoming, with Kelly community in foreground.

Sehr langsam und andächtig (♩=ca. 40)

First Notice to Friends

January 7

Sent via email to friends not yet contacted by phone.

Dear Friends and Companions,

My beloved husband, Jeffrey Joel, died in his bed while asleep at approximately 6:30 A.M., January 4, 2003 of an apparent heart attack. He was fifty-five years old.

His last three months were spent doing exactly what he wanted to do, which was to return to school, and take a law degree. We moved to Bloomington, Indiana for that purpose, and every morning he would leave the house with thirty pounds of books in his backpack, beaming with pleasure. The man truly loved to study. He was an eternal student, sensing the connections among widely various facts and impressions and beliefs, seeking to embrace and comprehend the whole.

The two weeks prior to Jeff's death felt like divine choreography. He visited with me in Massachusetts, where I was spending the winter with my children and grandchildren so as not to distract him with my presence during the first year of law school. He bonded with my two-year-old granddaughter Kiera in an extraordinary way, the two of them spending three days in his immense, increasingly spacious and sunny embrace.

In his final lunch with his father, a few days later in

New Jersey, Jeff told Amos that he loved him.

Many people remarked on the increase in luminosity shining from his face towards the end, the spaciousness, the immense relaxation into his essential being.

Our final evening together was full of joy and gentle joking, extraordinarily affectionate and loving.

I sense that he had achieved the purpose of his life: to open his emotional and spiritual heart so completely that his physical heart burst open, releasing him to the vast universe that had always been his true home.

Several people have remarked, in the days since, of a vision of Jeff streaking through the sky in a long robe (I had dressed his body in a long robe after washing and anointing it with essential oils), grey curls streaming behind, giggling with joy. His exhilaration is palpable.

I am left in shock, both ecstatic and grief-stricken. And so very thankful to the universe for gifting me with this great soul for the twelve short final years of his life on this Earth. He is one of the Ancient Ones. I sense his immense compassion and gentleness working to heal the interdimensional planes during this sacred terrible time of climactic violence on our beautiful green home planet.

May we all be gifted with such grace in our passing.

Jeffrey Joel, 1947–2003

Published in the Jackson Hole News and Guide *(Jackson, Wyoming) on January 22, 2003 under the title "Joel, fifty-five, healed on interdimensional planes," with subtitles chosen by the newspaper.*

Kelly Scholar had tremendous powers of concentration

Jeffrey Joel arrived in Jackson in the summer of 1990. He was a large, ungainly, sloppily dressed middle-aged man with a Buddha belly; that body and its fluid motion plus my imagined version of his intelligence reminded me of a dolphin. With grey/white hair corkscrewing out like it was transmitting permanent voltage from his giant bald egghead, he certainly stuck out in this hard-body town! My friends did not know what to make of him and I was embarrassed to be seen with him.

Our relationship did not begin with romance, it began in shadow. What most couples discover with a shock after romance has cooled, we ran into like a brick wall from the beginning. How did we survive it?

How did we even begin? Well, it all started on a shuttle bus on the way from the San Francisco airport to a hotel where we were both to attend a conference on "Cycles and Symbols." Most of the participants were astrologers like me, with an interest in psychology.

I have often told the story of how I instantly

"recognized his ass" (because I hadn't yet seen his face!) as he climbed up the shuttle's stairs in front of me. This man, I knew, was in my tribe. The shuttle was empty but for one other man, and as I watched them interact I was instantly repelled. In a contemptuous tone, Jeff said he was a mathematician, and that he was "slumming" at this conference on his way to a meeting on "Alchemical Hypnotherapy," one of his many healing modalities.

Absorbed knowledge from everywhere

Despite the off-putting start, that proved to be a turning-point weekend, full of synchronicities. It was a large conference, with over 700 attendees, and Jeff and I kept bumping into each other. Finally the two of us gave in, started talking. I discovered that he was trained at both Princeton and MIT, was a musician as well as mathematician, that he knew languages, that he was interested in just about everything, and carried both computer and encyclopedia in his head. However, I had to work to get him to speak above a mumble, and noticed his sometimes painfully shy, stuttering self-consciousness. And I was very judgmental about his overweight condition, preaching to him about diet, nutrition, exercise, etc.

That's when I saw him as a dolphin—not just his body, but his mind. I told him it seemed to me that he absorbed knowledge from all directions using sonar, sensing the fluid within which all things took place.

He liked that. He was a Leo, and loved being appreciated.

After the conference, he and I spent a night together at my friend Ella's home nearby, and then in the morning he went on his way.

I wanted to go to the ocean before flying back to

Jackson. So Ella drove me to a beach, where we walked along the Pacific tide line. I had my glasses in my hand so as to feel the salty air with my eyes. Suddenly Ella said, "Look, Annie!" pointing out to sea.

I put my glasses on and looked to where she was pointing. An entire pod of dolphins was cavorting there, just beyond the breakwater. They followed us up and down the beach for the next hour. Ella was astonished. She had never before seen dolphins at that particular beach.

That was the first of several miracles, which guided and affirmed my choice of partnering with this unusual urbane yet uncivilized man.

Bored with Mathematical Reviews

The second was a few weeks later, at another astrology conference at which I was again presenting. I had, foolishly, I thought, left a message on his answering machine, daring him to come live with me for a year rather than go to Atlanta for his sabbatical. (When I met him he had been for seventeen years an editor for *Mathematical Reviews*, an international journal in Ann Arbor, Michigan, and was, he said, "bored.")

I had left that message, and afterward felt terrified that he would take me up on it. Would I be willing to make room for a giant amoeba in my twenty-foot-diameter yurt?

It was at the end of that second conference when the second miracle occurred. I was sitting across from two people, one of them a close friend of mine. They were engrossed in conversation, and I was slumped in an exhausted stupor. At one point, the woman I did not know said, "When the teacher is tired, it's time to become a student again." At this, I involuntarily flinched and sighed "Ah, yes," recognizing its truth for me. Suddenly she turned 90° to face me and said, "I thought you would say that!"

She then proceeded, in a rapid monotone: "You have met a being. He is *huge*!" At this, I was startled, and shrunk back in alarm. She leaned forward. "And his *feet* are huge. He wears Birkenstocks, exactly like yours, only they're *suede*!" As this was a detail that Jeff and I had commented upon, I suddenly woke up to what she was saying. She went on to speak of him as a "star being from the Pleiades, connected to dolphin energy." She said that the two of us had work to do, that we would "anchor the northeast corner of a grid." (I still have no idea what that meant, though Jeff did not seem puzzled when told.)

Needless to say, I was blown away. From that moment on, no matter how bad things got between us—and at first they were terrible, two giant egos clashing, me determined to change him, him determined to resist—I would remember the miracles, and endure his sloth, his passive aggression, his rare but roaring anger.

A vast being

I'll never forget the day I stood outside the yurt, with him inside and massively depressed; I was yelling: "You asshole! I'm not going to kick you out!" (*He* had to make the decision to stay with me or not. I wasn't going to give him the opportunity to slink back to Michigan, tail between legs, feeling sorry for himself.)

Or the day when we were in Albertson's, and I noticed a young, mousey, sensitive woman whom I knew we couldn't avoid without being rude. With trepidation, in a quavering voice, I introduced him to her.

"Deb, this is Jeff."

He slouched up to her face and rudely roared:

"Hello!"

She shrunk back in alarm.

I was furious, and, once in the car, yelled at him all the way back home to Kelly, with him slouching further and further down, sunk in self-loathing.

When we got there, I could not stomach the idea of being in the yurt with him. It was one of those crystal blue -20°F days. I pulled a scarf over my mouth and started walking to the Warm Springs north of Kelly. There, I sat on a hillock which had been steamed free of snow, and watched the sun set through the mist. By the time I walked back, I knew something within me had shifted.

I opened the door and there he was, just the way I had left him, sitting on the couch, elbows on knees, holding his head. It looked like he weighed a thousand pounds; the usual depression, magnified.

I walked up, knelt down in front of him, and these words, startling even to me, poured out: "I am so grateful to be in this dance with you."

Jeff looked up at me, the surprise and wonder on his face mirroring my own. I proceeded to say how much I appreciated his very being. That his being was vast. That though my personality might be more socialized, my being was miniscule compared to his. That I could learn from him.

"Can I have a hug?"

And that's how it started. From then on, we were mindful of that distinction. Two people were involved in this relationship, and each had two aspects, persona and soul. We sensed that our connection was at a soul level, or we wouldn't be together, and that our difficulties were those of two personas, two egos who, both being stubborn and prideful, clashed.

Whenever we fought, sooner or later we remembered to look in each other's eyes, to see through persona to soul. And we made it a practice to ask the other, in the very moment of being most furious and frozen, most likely to walk away, "Can I have a hug?" I initiated this ritual, and he was always very willing to pull me into his embrace, relieved to have been forgiven.

By the end of our years together, this man with five planets in Leo had actually learned to apologize!

I have never met a man who was more willing to change—not to meet my needs, but to hear my truth, and allow it to affect his being. Because he was so resistant to my preaching, I was faced with an exacting mirror. Over and over again, his resistance reminded me to let go of my dogmatic Sagittarian ways, to simply speak my truth from my soul (which signaled its presence when my voice slowed, and dropped an octave), and then to simply let him go. To let go of all expectation as to how he would respond. I had to actually be willing for him to leave me, if necessary.

Over time, I grew to trust that Jeff would respond, because he always did, in his own way; at first it was days later, and then as time went on, and he began to learn that I truly did forgive him, it would take only hours, or even minutes, for him to surrender ego to soul.

The work we did in the outer world, initiating the Jackson Holistic Center as a clearinghouse for alternative thought and co-publishing *Crone Chronicles: A Journal of Conscious Aging*, were outgrowths of that inner work. How to see through persona to soul. How to allow the magnetic connection between us to flower in the world.

Emerging from depression

The resulting transformation, in both of us, was subtle, steady, and total. Within a few years Jeffrey was emerging from depression. He began to sense the wildness within himself in this wild place, to look forward to chopping wood and carrying water at the yurt, to relish skiing and walking in the mountains, and to pursue his beloved swimming on a near-daily basis. His rough persona eased into a gentleness and caring from which many people received the benefits. They sensed an attentive ear and sympathetic eye, and some even surrendered to his increasingly large-hearted embrace.

His interests, as many people know, were both extremely varied, and pursued in depth. He was a true Renaissance man in an age of specialists; a polyglot polymath in an age of narrow linear thought. He had two calling cards, one left-brained, and one right-brained; the latter he labeled, accurately, "Circumconscious Navigations." Periodically, people—especially other body workers—would come to him for Trager bodywork, for which he had trained and had become a tutor, and had even organized and incorporated the International Trager Association. Once in a while someone would call for a hypnotherapy session with him, though their presenting problem, usually addiction, he would tell them might not be healed through hypnosis.

He was always reading widely and deeply. His office was so disgustingly cluttered that it reminded me of a giant bird's nest: a chaotic mixture of papers, books, magazines and junk mail curving steadily up, with a narrow trail from doorway to computer.

Generous oaf was sensitive to touch

Jeff could sit for hours at a time, translating mathematics for German and Russian publishers while listening to opera in another language, singing along. He multitracked easily within, but if I came in and touched his shoulder, wanting his attention, he would jump, furious. This big wonderful lazy generous preoccupied oaf was extremely sensitive to touch.

His tendrils reached into many areas of the community: into theater (where he played the Grandfather to Susan Juvelier's Grandmother in several *Nutcracker* productions) and music (he was in the choir, and a great friend of both choirmaster Bob Partridge and composer George Hufsmith). He was one of the Geologists of Jackson Hole, and loved their noon meetings on scientific subjects. He was, for a time, on the Public Lands Committee of the Jackson Hole Alliance, and was one of the founders and the incorporator of the Jewish Community of Jackson Hole.

His work with *Crone Chronicles*—which carried clout nationally way in excess of its miniscule print run, having been nominated for *Utne Reader* Alternative Awards several times, and featured in many big city dailies and on ABC's "Good Morning America"—was thankless, as some female subscribers were upset to hear a man even answer the phone. This pained both of us. But Jeff soldiered on, bailing out the magazine with money whenever it threatened to go under. When I told him in September of 2000 that I was finished, that I was too exhausted to do another issue, he urged me to do two more issues: one to announce the decision to close, and another to give room for reader response. So that is what we did, finally closing the magazine with the Spring 2001 issue after twelve years.

Years earlier, I had promised that the next move was his, that it would be my turn to make up to him for his long years of sacrifice to my interests. Gleefully, he elected to go to law school, choosing Indiana University.

Last summer we moved to Bloomington, Indiana. When school started, every morning this brand-new, middle-aged pupil would leave the house with thirty pounds of books in his backpack, beaming with childlike pleasure. The man truly loved to study. He was an eternal student, sensing the connections between widely various facts and impressions and fields, seeking to embrace and comprehend the whole.

The two weeks prior to his death—from a heart attack while asleep on the morning of January 4, 2003— felt like divine choreography.

He was fifty-five years old. He is one of the Ancient Ones.

Jeff is survived by his father, Amos Joel, of Maplewood, N.J., and his sisters, Stephanie Joel, of New York City, and Andrea Joel, of Los Angeles. Please send any donations in his name to either the Jackson Hole Housing Trust or the Jewish Community of Jackson Hole. The Jewish Community will host a Celebration of Jeffrey Joel's life in early June.

Indiana School of Law Memorial

January 22

> *I wrote the following report to give Jeff's dad and sisters some flavor of the Law School memorial held at IU on January 21, 2003. Jeff had been a first-year law student there when he died, just prior to the opening of the second semester.*

Yesterday I attended the memorial held in Jeffrey's memory which had been called by Len Fromme, the Dean of Students at the Law School of Indiana University.

Because Dean Fromme assumed that not many people had known Jeff, the event was held in the Faculty Lounge. This room turned out to be too small for the fifty or so people that crowded in to hear each other's stories of how their lives had been touched by this unusual man who was with them for such a short time and whose impact, everyone agreed, had been profound.

At first, as people were coming in, the atmosphere felt heavy, funereal. To me, it felt like they were all treading gingerly, embarrassed to be in my presence, thinking I must be so depressed by my loss. Finally, I said, out of the blue, "You know, Jeff was not a solemn person!" That broke the ice; everyone laughed in relief.

Dean Fromme started off listing a few things from Jeff's resume, just to give the students and professors and deans gathered an idea of Jeff's rich background, the variety of situations and learning experiences he had incorporated before arriving at IU. The dean said that on a personal note, he had been amazed by just how wide Jeff's knowledge was. One day a Russian student was in his office when Jeff walked in. The girl seemed ill at ease and timid. Jeff asked her where she was from. She mentioned a little town in Russia. He said, "Oh, I know where that is, it's about an eight-hour train ride from Moscow, right?" She was flabbergasted, as was the dean. He then told us how he would run into Jeff in the hallways, and always some conversation ensued in which Dean Fromme learned something, some insight or way of seeing something, which he had not thought of before.

As soon as he finished, the Dean of Admissions stood up and rushed to the podium, to tell us of how he had recruited Jeffrey, whose resume had impressed him so thoroughly. Then, when Jeff agreed to come here, Dean Robles said, "I crowed to everyone I met, 'I just got me my own Princeton mathematician!'" (He had just been to see the movie, *A Beautiful Mind*.) This was a wonderful, lighthearted moment.

Like Dean Fromme, Dean Robles would also run into Jeff in the hallway. "But," he said, "not just the hallway, but everywhere. He was everywhere! I'd see him down in the basement; next I'd be in the library, and there he was! Then I'd be up on the third floor, again, there was Jeffrey!"

One of the students corroborated that sensation of Jeff being everywhere. And he went on to say, "Everybody around here is scurrying fast, heads down, like busy little bees; but not Jeff! I'd see him ambling down the hall in his own slow, measured pace, and he always had time to stop and talk. And when he talked with you, he listened intently to what *you* had to say. He wasn't just pretending to listen while impatient to be rushing off to the next class. And even though I thought I needed to rush, I always stayed to talk, because it was so interesting. Jeffrey helped me learn how to be in the moment. To be fully present for whatever was happening."

Several students spoke of his "humility," his desire to "share knowledge," his "large, open mind." One remarked, "He was "so open and patient and serene; he had the qualities of a sage." This same student had just founded a "Constitutional Society," and Jeff had volunteered to help write its by-laws over Thanksgiving. Then the student discovered that they couldn't get a grant for it until the end of the second semester. "So I told Jeff that we would have to wait to write the by-laws. I was relieved at the delay, because I was so busy, but Jeff, who was just as busy, was disappointed!" Another lighthearted moment.

Several pointed out how many different student activities Jeff had participated in, including the forum on Feminist Law, and the one that helped battered women and children. He had even gone out with students one night to their local joint for a beer.

Students and teachers who had been in classes with him remarked on how lively he was in class, on how he always had something to say, some new way of looking at a situation, or new way of thinking about things.

Jeffrey's "Contracts" professor, an older man who is semi-retired, told me personally that he had had many long talks with Jeffrey on many subjects, and remarked that he was a "wonderful man." He seemed unusually stricken by Jeff's sudden death, and my new friend Herb (Jeff's old student friend from Princeton, an IU professor of English) said that one of this Contracts teacher's students told him that yesterday had been their first class of this semester, and that the professor had started off talking about Jeffrey, and that he had been obviously very moved by losing Jeff, so much so that he had trouble getting back to the subject of Contracts.

Over and over again, I heard how "present" Jeff was, how always serene and happy, how he "magnetized people with his presence."

One student talked about how they had once talked about how she loved snow, and that the first day it snowed this winter he had emailed her about it, saying that he hoped she was happy, because it had snowed!

Another student talked about how Jeffrey had told her he worried that "he took up too much space." She was speaking on a physical level, in terms of his large body, but I and others felt the poignancy of this remark. He was such a vast being internally, and had such trouble finding a way to nestle his full self within this narrow-minded society.

Several students mentioned how he taught them to "just do it, whatever it is!"—that his going back to law school in his fifties as one of a long list of changes throughout his life was inspiring to them.

I told them one story.

About six months ago, I noticed that my perspective on the world was changing. My former polarized views of things were dissolving. I no longer saw myself as on the side of the "righteous" as opposed to my "enemies," which for me had been Bush, Cheney and Rumsfeld. I was beginning to sense the field in which we were all playing, that all of us were in a great drama in which we were each taking certain parts, from our own perspective and to the best of our abilities. That each of us is doing the best we can. That there are no enemies, and no polarization, either.

Jeff listened to me, and then, in the low, slow voice that signaled his soul speaking to mine, uttered these words: "Yes. And I think that is the beginning of cosmic consciousness." (He said this as if in an offhand manner, then immediately walked out of the room.)

It took me twelve years to learn this lesson, this letting go of judgment, and simply bearing witness to events with compassion. Jeff graciously remained by my side until I had learned it.

This story, which had me in tears, opened a floodgate of remarks from students, who said that he had also taught them to take things in without judging them. That his way of being was like that of a child, that he held such an openness and such a curiosity about what life has to offer that it was very inspiring to them. One student capped it off for all of us: "I started out being impressed by Jeffrey's huge brain; I ended up thinking of him as an astonishing human being."

Sisterhood

January 27

This chapter was first published in the Summer 2003 edition of SageWoman Magazine, *where I have been a regular columnist since 1995.*

I have just picked up a jar; then I turn quickly, my arm flying out. The cap on the jar flies off, spilling sauce onto the rug. Instantly, three women wet cloths with water and kneel to remove the stains.

That response, that immediate noticing of what I needed as if it were the finale of the same motion that produced the need: how can I describe my gratitude? It was as if these three women were the embodiment of the Triple Goddess herself, cradling me in her many arms.

My husband had died one week prior—in the early morning of a heart attack while asleep. This sudden loss, which hurled a thousand-pound weight into heart and belly, was now being dreamily if temporarily cushioned by sisterhood, this ancient global community of women who sustain each other in birth and death and transitions in between.

On January 4, 2003 I arose from sleep at around 8:30 in the morning. On my way down the hall to the kitchen, I passed by Jeff's bedroom's open doorway, and, repeating the half-conscious daily ritual following his first heart attack five years ago, paused briefly to be reassured by the sound of his breathing. How many times had I imagined the day when the body would be still, when the breath no longer rose and fell in that large hairy chest? How many times had I rehearsed time's slowing down, that long walk to his bedside, my stunned stare at the familiar face, now strange.

The eyes and mouth were half-open; the skin a mottled blue-grey.

I could feel my mind skitter as my eyes jerked, back and forth, up and down. Ach! Suddenly all the rehearsals had yielded this performance, this *reality*. Jeffrey, my beloved husband of twelve years, was dead. *Dead*. Not here. Not in his body. The body was stone still; though the fold in his neck was warm, his hands and arms were chilled.

I can see now that all those rehearsals were an unconscious attempt to inoculate myself against horrific shock.

Of course the attempt failed.

I thought I knew shock. At times I've even billed myself as a sort of shock expert, a shock therapist. But I did *not* know shock. Nor did I anticipate how my own body would flash freeze in the same instant my mind shot out in startled panic.

I've always wondered how I would react in an emergency not yet faced. Looking back, I feel somewhat surprised, given my penchant for solitude and self-reliance, that what I wanted, needed, most right then and there was a woman's hand, a woman's touch, her calm and reassuring presence.

And here's the rub. I was in Bloomington, Indiana, thousands of miles from both my blood sisters and long-time female friends, most of whom lived in Jackson, Wyoming, the town from which Jeff and I had moved, only four months earlier.

I was in a new town. And my husband had just died.

Oddly enough, by the munificent grace of the Goddess, I knew exactly who to contact. I was *not* alone. Herb and Perry arrived twenty minutes later, and spent the entire day with me. I "slept" at their house that night and the next, and they have basically been on call for me ever since.

I say "slept" in quotes, because that first night was entirely sleepless; an eight-hour-hyperaware-vigil-staring-into-the-void; I was in limbo, suspended between heaven and earth, unable to rise and join him in his joy nor to descend into the familiar comfort of earth: that First Night, without a wink of sleep, eyelids closed and eyeballs behind them a startled-endless-wide-awake was, I can name it now, The Agony.

Looking back, I realize that this couple's arrival the morning Jeff died had been set in motion four months earlier. We had invited them for dinner and I greeted them at the door. As Perry crossed over the threshold my eyes shyly sought hers, and then suffered a sudden shearing, the moment splitting into before and after: for there she was, this large vulnerable soul I remembered—from where? And how long ago? As I remarked to Jeff later, while washing dishes and still enveloped in that rare, full feeling of group camaraderie, "Perry is utterly familiar; I *know* her."

And now here she was, four months later, once again crossing our threshold with her husband Herb to support me on the morning that my husband had suddenly, shockingly, died.

I now sense that first evening encounter with Perry as the opening note of a divine choreography, so much do I honor the perfection in the process of Jeff's long, slow release from this life and embrace of the next.

I call it a "long, slow release," because, though he died suddenly, there had been clues in the months prior that something miraculous was afoot. Jeff had been deliriously happy to be back in school at the ripe age of fifty-five, learning yet another new language, the language of the law. Then, on vacation with me in Massachusetts for Christmas, he had been in an astonishingly open, expanded state while sitting Buddha-like on the floor and quietly following the quixotic lead of my two-year-old granddaughter, Kiera; her very own "Papa Jeff." A few days later, he told his father that he loved him after their last lunch together in New Jersey on his way back to Bloomington. After his emergency angioplasty on January 2, I had walked into his hospital room (having flown immediately from Massachusetts) and discovered him still expanded, serene, illumined—decidedly atypical behavior for a heart patient. Finally, our last evening together on January 3, only hours before he died, played out truly as the finale, a time of playful affection, hanging out on our big old couch together, rubbing and touching and gently joking, murmuring "I love you. . . ."

Now, in the early morning of the very next day, I discover he is dead. And, after that first half-hour of total panic and confusion, I have called in my new friends, Herb and Perry, both professors at Indiana University. Herb had been a classmate of Jeff's at Princeton, over thirty years ago. When Jeff decided to come here to law school he contacted Herb, and they renewed their friendship. That first magical dinner with them, soon after I arrived in town, was followed by other dinners, especially after I left again—at Jeff's request; he wanted solitude during his first year in law school—to spend the winter in Massachusetts with my children and grandchildren.

And now, within minutes, they responded to my

call on a morning that signified both the end of my familiar life and Day One of an unknown future. What were the protocols for this day? What to do, when?

Herb took charge of finding a compatible firm for cremation and for issuing the death certificate. Perry took charge of me, sitting by my side as my system reacted to the thudding reverberations of shock, keening loudly and wildly, mouth stretched into a giant "O." And she held me as I rocked myself, trying vainly for the comfort that only his body could give. And she sat quietly and with full presence as I chaotically paced the floor, rubbed my face, rushed to the bathroom with runaway diarrhea.

I then asked Herb to go home and find appropriate books for us to read from in a private ceremony for Jeff; I wanted an eclectic service that would include major religions without adhering to any of them. He returned with the Bible, the *Tibetan Book of the Dead*, and the traditional Jewish Siddur. We made an altar on a beautiful Buddhist prayer rug and placed a candle in the middle with photos of Jeff around it, interspersed with his crystals and little Inuit animal sculptures. Then the three of us sat in a triangle around the altar and meditated; we read to each other from the Psalms, from the Bardo for those who have recently passed over, and recited Kaddish. And we each spoke of Jeff, who he was for us, his effect on our lives, our great love for him.

Herb had arranged for the cremation people to come at 4:00 P.M., so that there would be time to wash Jeff's body and for me to spend some time alone with him.

Neither Perry nor I had ever washed a dead body before. Yet I knew we were meant to do this. Such an age-old ritual felt totally familiar. And doing it with another woman felt absolutely right, essential.

We washed his body with soap and water, then

rinsed him with water diluted with essential oils of sandalwood, sage and juniper; finally, we dressed him in a beautiful long robe. I had asked Herb to read poetry during this ceremony. Since most of Jeff's little sculptures were of animals, Herb decided to read from the "Jubilate Agno" by Christopher Smart, a poem that celebrates the atonement of all nations, languages and creatures, and takes joy in the antics of the author's cat named "Jeoffrey." Naturally, one of our cats chose that time to enter the room and cavort among us for the entire washing ceremony.

I swear I could feel a smile on Jeff's face, too, as Felix jumped up on the bed, casually sniffed his body, jumped in front of the book Herb was reading from, and just generally had a very good time.

That feeling, of having a very good time, was a subset to what I can only describe as a species of ecstasy to which I had gradually surrendered as the day went along. I sensed my own participation in Jeff's awe and wonder at the indescribable beauty of worlds beyond. (And yet, for the next three days, I was also, like a child who has had a numinous experience, afraid of the dark; for once I did not force myself, like the good little soldier I have been all my life, to confront this fear and march myself down into the basement. Instead, I allowed the fear, watched it like a mother would watch her child until the fear dissolved.)

Of course I was on the phone the next three days, responding to the grief and shock of friends, mostly women, a number of whom said they would drop everything and fly to my side, should I say the word. I did choose two for this comfort: my sister, Kathy, and my dearest friend, Claudia, both of Seattle. They helped me bundle his clothes for Goodwill, clear out his law books for resale, clean up his room and his office so that I could move into them. Then, on the day before these two loving beings were to depart, we invited Perry over for lunch. That was when I whirled around and the cap to the sauce flew off and they were all right there, responding to my need. For over two hours the four of us sat on the living room floor bathed in winter sunlight subtly sifting through diaphanous curtains. We were quietly, with full attention, listening to each other's lives. We were doing what women, everywhere, do. Being women in community, present for each other, both witnessing and participating in the joys and sorrows of the days and hours.

I cannot thank them enough for their presence in my life as I walk into the Great Unknown.

Response to Friends

February 28

For those who sent condolences via snail mail.

Dear

Thanks for being there. I feel your energy buoying me up as I sense my way through these long days and nights. Waves of grief move through like tsunamis, sometimes every three days, sometimes on successive days, sometimes not appearing for a week or so. Through each descent into mourning, I seem to contact, release, and then refresh yet another and deeper layer of communion with my dear man no longer in form but so very present! And in between the spasms of grieving come moments of indescribable beauty and joy.

I work on projects—understanding finances (that was his department); unpacking and deciding what books to keep from his 250 boxes stored in the basement; reading up on and experimenting with the way my new computer works (he was also my tech support guy).

All these projects, which used to "bore" me, projects that I thought too trivial to merit my attention, slow me to a snail's crawl, which is where I must be emotionally to process this strange, powerful, and unforeseen period in a usually pell-mell life.

The kitties keep me warm. This little house feels safe and comforting. Bloomington is a rich new place to explore and meet like-minded people. And every early morning, moving through tai chi, I am cheered by birds calling out Spring! through the still bare branches.

All my love to you,

Phenomena

Early April

> *My late husband, Jeffrey Joel, sometimes told me he could see space ships hiding in clouds over the Tetons. He would point out the presence of energy vortices, as well as of fairies, elves and other spirit beings in nature. And he told stories of strange encounters, like the time when he awakened from a dream of being in the Kalahari desert with a shaman to discover his hiking boots, which he kept in his closet, by the front door covered with clay.*
>
> *I was, of course, always astonished and intrigued by these experiences, and would beg for more. He would wave me off, dismissing them as unimportant, "mere phenomena." Thus this chapter's title.*
>
> *I imagine that everyone who knew Jeff would agree that he was an unusual man. This story, of the "phenomena" which trailed his departure like phosphorescence in a heaving sea, continues that unusual legacy.*

Death of a loved one releases energy. As spirit rushes from its binding in material form, shock waves spread into family and community. Through phone lines and email the waves radiate in widening circles; within twenty-four hours most of those who knew him or her suffer the sudden halt of daily busyness. Minds lunge to grasp the new reality; hearts open fully, if briefly, to listen to what is and is not of value.

And if death releases energy, then sudden, unexpected death is a cataclysmic event. Our ordinary worlds stop cold. Wind rushes in to announce the presence of Mystery.

It has been three months since Jeff died. Since then, my entire life has been lifted into the invisible arms of my beloved. This may sound like metaphoric flight, the sincere but temporary teary-eyed sentiment of a grieving widow. It is not: I sit cradled in the void that holds the slow whirling of death and life.

All my life I have longed to be worthy of the attention of one of humanity's archetypes: this is the Death Goddess, the Great Crone Herself, in whose honor Jeff and I published a small but potent magazine, *Crone Chronicles, A Journal of Conscious Aging*, for twelve long years.

It turns out the Crone was stalking me; Jeff's death ushered Her in, full-blown. This essay is a commentary on the slow sure ways She lets us in on the omnivorous nature of the Real.

For me, the interval between that early morning shock of discovering his lifeless body on the bed and my personal absorption of this new reality has a peculiar ontological feel. Both space and time are affected. I experience Space as if there has been a shearing of two tectonic plates, each upholding a separate world. Between the two plates is a narrow path which, if I hold a focus, I can use to go back and forth between his world and my own. And Time? It not only "flies" and "crawls"—as the usual metaphors suggest—but Time now bumps along in a descending series of thudding jolts.

With each jolt I sense an even deeper tier of the matrix, which held us, evaporate. I marvel and weep at each new recognition of just how profoundly multilayered, how textured and nuanced, was our bond. Correction: *is* our bond. For the path between worlds remains. And each dissolution carves away the trappings of form to reveal the essence of spirit. As I surrender the hooks coupling my personality to his, so the soul within each of us comes forward. My unconscious works mightily to let go of attachment to Jeff's incarnated self, while simultaneously, my heart opens to the presence of the Love in which my being is held. There is no net loss. There is, in fact, a subtle and all-pervasive gain. I sit inside the fragrant garden of divine abundance.

This, too, may sound like a flight of fancy, but be assured that, on the mundane level, at hourly, daily, weekly, monthly—irregularly spaced but sharp—intervals, over and over I still find myself coming up out of whatever daily task I am engaged in to stare in the mirror of this unfamiliar new reality. "What?" I internally shout, bereft, disbelieving. "No! It can't be true!"

But it is. It always is. Over and over again, it is true. His car still sits in the driveway, but that does not mean Jeff is home to greet me. His bathrobe hangs from the hook next to mine, and will not leave that hook again until I personally remove it. The rest of his clothes are gone, but his beloved mathematical, musical, scientific, literary, political, psychological, sociological, shamanistic, and metaphysical books in many different languages (250 boxes), not to mention his classical, oriental, Native American, music tapes and CDs (30 boxes), his medicine bag and pipe, his skis and snowshoes and bike—all hunker in the basement, awaiting dispersal to new homes.

Yes. He is indeed gone and he left me to deal with a mountain of stuff. His stuff. That he was so excessive in all directions was by far the biggest "issue" for me in our relationship. I am by nature abstemious and somewhat austere, and was overwhelmed by our slow, insidious immersion in more and more stuff—and told him so, many times. I instinctively knew that I would be the one who would have to deal with the stuff in the end—and told him that too, vehement. The very thought of having to plough through his rich morass exhausted me. Had I known myself better when he was alive, I would have noticed that those fleeting premonitions of having to work with his remains rendered me desolate.

But the books and the music were Jeff's friends, perhaps his closest friends, as I realize now. And during the two-month-long post-mortem project of sorting—deciding what to keep and what to recycle, what to give to friends and family, what to sell and donate—I found myself actually enjoying this belated plunge into his emotional, mental and spiritual range and depth. I felt like a child unwrapping Christmas presents, the contents of each box a magical mystery tour. What would I find now? What would make me stop in my tracks, to read?

Thus what had been our biggest stumbling block transformed into the gift of his munificence to me. Even in death, he was my teacher.

Going through the stuff also kept him tangibly here.

But this job is now done, and he's still not gone. Indeed, he's more present than ever. I feel closer to him now than while he was in human form, because I always sensed him holding his essential self closely, protecting himself, hiding even from me—or, maybe, especially from me.

While in body, many could sense that Jeff felt

constrained, held down, held back, his large brooding
spirit dragging around that heavily muscled, big-bellied
body scarred from all those colon operations, those heart
attacks. Like his mother, he was embarrassed about his
size. Both were Leos who wore their shadows on the
outside, their dense physical encumbrances embedding the
splendor of ancient souls.

He kept trying to make himself smaller, to conform
to standard taste. I exhorted him to glory in his immensity,
to discard tight clothes, to wear loose shirts and pants! To
even dare to wear long robes, to dress like the king that
he was! (Remember! I would admonish him. Your Sun is
at the 29th degree of Leo, conjunct Regulus!) Of course
he dismissed this idea with a snort, while carefully and
obsessively measuring tiny gains and losses via the notches
on his belt.

Angele, one of the more metaphysical people in
our community of souls, lives on top of a mountain near
Los Alamos, meditating on war and peace. She called to
console me a few days after he died. I told her that his
cremation would be the next day, and she said, "When?
Because I want to go into meditation during that time."

Two months later, we spoke again. She told me
she had stayed in meditation for the entire four hours of
his cremation and had the distinct feeling that he caused
his own body to flash into fire, through spontaneous
combustion, that "though there might have been something
mechanical going on also, he was in charge."

She then told me that more recently, during a
candlelit dinner with her husband, she happened to
glance at the flame and noticed a tiny being emerging
and disappearing, like Aladdin from his lamp. At first she
thought it must be a nature spirit, as she had been recently
working with them. But the little creature kept whooshing

in and out—until she noticed that he was bald, with white corkscrew curls, and wearing a long robe. (I had dressed him in a long robe after tenderly washing his dead body.) Suddenly she knew—it was Jeff!—insistently passing in and out of the flame until she recognized him. "And I got the distinct impression," she told me, laughing, "that he *loved* being small. Now that he is out of material form, he is free to be any size he wishes!"

Angele and I have never before talked by phone. Yet her reaching out to me was not unusual. For not only did my dear companion leave me, his father and sisters, and his many friends from many different communities behind, but I notice since then that the linkages among some of us were abruptly shattered and often, just as abruptly reconstituted—but deeper, more heartfelt. Others, like Angele, have connected with me for the first time, after years of honoring each other from a distance.

In Jeff's death bloomed paradox, for it was his sudden absence that announced the magnitude of his living presence. We are finally discovering who he was, or at least we are acknowledging how much his usually silent observant awareness meant to us. His death brought us closer in life; we feel vulnerable, and hold tenderly those who remain.

For if any death releases energy, and if, moreover, sudden death is a cataclysmic event, then the leap from incarnation of a great soul like Jeffrey is a clarion call to all creation. As we, in our grieving, seek to keep him here through memory, we start to recall and tell each other stories which glimpse aspects of his multifaceted reality— only to come away astonished and disturbed by how much we did *not* know. We discover that each of us was graced with a tiny piece of the puzzle that was his vast being on this earth; that each of us interacted with a man who was so full and so large that he had room for all our quirks; he could meet us there, wherever we were, and be glad. Jeffrey was a giant sponge, absorbing the joys and pains of our world; he was a watcher, overlooking the action while smiling inside, as meanwhile he was being called, forever called, into other worlds to which only he was privy.

I was with him for twelve short years, and in the rare early mornings when he'd awaken to tell me he'd remembered a dream from the night before, I would eagerly ask about it. "Why do you want to know?" he would say, amused, or even annoyed. "Because I need clues as to you are," I would respond coyly, pretending a casualness I did not feel. (I always felt like a pipsqueak next to him.) Again, he would dismiss my need to know him as one more symptom of my "lack of boundaries."

That First Night after he died was agony, a peculiar sense of being suspended between heaven and earth and unable to access either. As the weeks roll on, this space of suspension has become my treasured home, a soft, safe place hidden from prying eyes. I discover that literally hundreds of people care for me, but no one really needs, nor do they ask, to know in detail what I am going through. This zone of privacy, this very intimate environment in which I am allowed to process and integrate loss, is a wonderful gift.

Yes, I am still suspended, and now this state of being feels good. I remain in the little home in Bloomington we shared for such a short time before he died. Every day I begin with yoga, chi kung and tai chi. I move through this ritual to center and strengthen my energy, so that I can more fully appreciate the present—the extraordinary gift— of the here and now.

And though I remain suspended, and though my experience of space and time has altered to reflect the new context, I now notice that the boundaries between heaven and earth—between this dimension and other, wilder, ones—continuously disintegrate. And here is where, I suppose, I might (finally!) begin to focus fully on the story of the "phenomena" attending his death. For as my reality shifts I discover that "above" and "below" are not separate, but intermingled; they swirl. I have abandoned my usual press-forward-ahead orientation. I am lost in Mystery, and paradoxically, I feel I have finally been found.

I sense my awareness simultaneously creating and exploring a space in which the essence of both Jeff and myself can play, indeed a space that *is* the essence of Jeff and *is* the essence of Ann. Not "together," but One. Not hand in hand, but inside each other, my soul in his, his in mine. "We" are the field in which my embodied being—my "personality"—plays. "I" am—my body is—the locus of our action in the world. Both feet on the ground, like a wedge, implanting other dimensions into this one.

(This new reality of interdimensional Oneness was made abundantly clear in a dream in which he and I were walking through a store pushing a shopping cart, buying food. It was the most ordinary of daily life routines. Suddenly, in the dream, I realized that I had been writing obits for him, and telling people he was dead—when he was not! In the dream I apologized to him profusely for this drastic mistake.)

The post-mortem surrender to Oneness has no definition and no edges. The very act of exploring itself pushes boundaries into the far distance where they turn porous and dissolve.

I am attempting to give form to the ineffable, to see into the void, to grasp and describe the nature of this brand new world into which his so-called "death" has shoved me. My attempts fail. The ineffable slips through my mind like our cat Felix flows from the reach of my seeking hands.

The edges of the world no longer exist. The edges of what I believe and don't believe, of the ideologies I used to hold, of my strongly-held ideas of right and wrong, blur. No matter how strong my personality's usual determination to keep them separate and divided, my heart opens to encompass them all. And if there were ever to be a test of my new and strange and unfamiliar compassion for all the players in any human drama, it is the so-called "second Gulf War on Iraq," blaring from TV and newspaper headlines. Though my awareness of humanity's latest tragedy moves me as usual to fury and fear, for the first time in a life filled with images of war's horror, I am not caught in polarity.

What has "caused" this change? How has Jeff's death worked such wonders in me? I bow before this mystery. And I recount for you here the marvels and miracles that have spiraled forth since that early morning when he suddenly and unexpectedly whooshed out of our shared earthly household.

On the third day after he died, I dreamed that he came to me in the guise of a beautiful young man. (I did not recognize his body, but knew it was him.) We were at a noisy party and he took me into a back room. There he told me (or I got the sense that he transmitted to me) that I was to be in school, and that this school would last for two months. I asked him if he was working on helping the Mideast, and got a surprising answer. "No!" he said, emphatically. "That is *old*."

At the time his remark was puzzling. But now—more than two months later—I sense what might be a glimmer of its meaning. This sense has come in through the way I have been living, which is to read the *New York Times* daily, and to watch the TV news nightly, and then, to put it all aside and bring Aloha to every moment of every day, to every person I meet, to the sun and sky and stars and the exhaust from all the cars. To settle into this one moment here, now, to follow the call of Beauty. To let the old world go and inaugurate the new.

There have been times when I have been puzzled by this response, by this decided bifurcation of worlds within me. For yes, I do wail and gnash my teeth in the face of the seeming stupidity and destructiveness of the world's power brokers. And yes, I do live in Beauty. Both are true. The one does not negate, but completes the other.

Thus do the polarities within me both increase their separate intensities while being mutually included in an even larger dimension, a transcendent field of joyous play. The field Jeff and I, as souls, as beings, essences, inhabit together, or rather, the dazzling, endlessly sparkling space being woven through this play.

The night after that first dream of Jeff I had another dream in which I was being escorted into dimensions Jeff now inhabits—a universe so beautiful and so thrilling that there is no way I can describe it. Indeed, because I cannot give words to it, I cannot remember it; I can only remember *that* I had the vision of splendor, not its content.

Even so, these two dreams announced the onset of a series of "events" (do I call them that, when they are in no way of this ordinary world?) that trailed his leaving like phosphorescence in the wake of his giant ship as it slipped, silent, into the approaching dawn.

There were those who, during the first few days after his departure, saw him in their mind's eye flying. . . . Scott: "Jeff was flying, laughing, with curly hair streaming out behind him. He was wearing a purple-pink thing."

Scott's wife, Todd, who receives information through automatic writing, said the word describing Jeff's passing was ". . . breathtaking. Literally, taking away the breath, as it was so dynamic."

She later emailed me a copy of what had come through her writing:

"Enormous!! Energy, sparkling free—couldn't contain it any longer. (It 'burst' upon him.) First, it's a pirouette, then the waltz, then marching band. (All music, enormous music.) This image is given over to the exploding clown at the circus, who turns into the monkey doing back flips onto the elephant trumpeting in full voice—Oh, my! (giggling uncontrollably). Trying to control the seriousness is important, but for the life (guffaw) of me, I can't get there'—to the seriousness.

"This is so much fun—I always wanted to do this consciously—and here it is—such immense pleasure, such boundless joy, such unspeakable truths, such (giggle again) unpronounceable words—no words—just unmitigated JOY—FUN exhilaration all running together—all over and through me—the Me that sparkles—jumble of sparkletts! Oh, the Beauty, the Exquisiteness! I'm finally speechless (giggle), at least for a while—this moment—but wait, I love you, dear Ann. (You are) the Light shining for me. I love your enormous sparkle, too! See, I can stay serious for less than a nanosecond—It's glorious! Later, later! . . .' (He's humming music!)"

The first notice that this was to be an unusual passing came within two hours of Jeff's death when my new Bloomington friends Herb and Perry did ceremony with me. (Herb and Jeff had known each other as Princeton undergraduates.) I created an altar on Jeff's Tibetan prayer rug with some of his crystals and little Inuit sculptures of animals and dolphins surrounding a candle. In honor of Jeff's embrace of all the world's religions, we planned to include psalms from the Bible and the Jewish Siddur;

we began by reading from the *Tibetan Book of the Dead*, thinking we were to help Jeff pass through the Bardo state into the light. Halfway through the reading we looked at each other and murmured, amazed: "Jeff doesn't need this." *We* needed it; *we* were the ones who were wandering in shadow, working with shock and pain and confusion, not him. Already, we were sensing his light, joyful, active presence in the room. Just then, a sudden gust activated the wind chimes outside the window. (Ever since then I hear these chimes as Jeff calling my name; they gently return me to the present from my wandering.)

A few days later I received this note via email from a friend, Cate, and her eight-year-old daughter, Stella, who had been our neighbors in the mountain village of Kelly, Wyoming:

"I burst into tears when I hung up the phone from Lyn's call with the news—and Stella came immediately to my side, embracing me legs to waist. She remembers Jeff well and after holding one another for a while we went outside in the morning air and called out his name to all of life here—West, South, East and North. Then Stella came back inside and on her own gathered every bison figure and image we have in the house and also a multitude of owls, setting them in a very specific arrangement on the kitchen table. We lit candles and kept his altar for several days. We also let animals we came in contact with over those several days hear of his change."

I replied: "Thank you so much for your vigil with the animals! Did you know that we created an altar here surrounded by his sculptures of animals, and that when my friend Perry and I washed Jeff's body, her husband Herb was reading a rollicking poem about animals and that Felix, one of our cats, cavorted among us for that whole ceremony? How wonderfully synchronous."

A few days later, another friend phoned to tell me of her experience upon hearing the news. She and her husband Tim were honeymooning on the island of Maui. Later, Deidre sent me the story via email:

"On January 4, 2003 Tim and I went to the Iao of the Needle, a sacred site on Maui known as the Burial Place of the Chiefs. We chose this place for our ceremony to release Jeff because of the beauty and power of the place, with a powerful altar used by locals, and because there is a huge feral community of cats there and I wanted to feed the cats in Jeff's name. Also, the idea of the burial place of the Chiefs attracted me as Jeff was a chief on all psychospiritual levels.

"We approached the altar which is directly in front of the rock/hill formation that is the Iao of the Needle, just at dusk. The sun was behind a cloud. I picked yellow daisies for Jeff.

"Tim sat on the ground facing the Needle and prayed. I held the daisies in front of the altar and closed my eyes. Immediately I was bathed in a beautiful golden/yellow light. I thought this was the power of suggestion from the yellow flowers but decided to work with the color. That golden color filled me and all my images of Jeff. I opened my eyes to look at the Needle as I prayed, and the sky had opened and the sun shined brightly on the rock formation. There was a lichen or some plant on the rocks that glowed a beautiful golden/yellow light. At that point I felt Jeff's presence very strongly. I spoke to him of the love I have for him and how I will miss him, and I wished him well and released him to the light. At that point he spoke to me in my head. I heard Jeff say very clearly, 'Please tell Ann I am sorry, I am sorry I did not call out to her to say good-bye. What I was experiencing was so beautiful; no words for it and I was in such awe of the experience that I allowed myself to simply be with it. There was no struggle. At some point I realized I was leaving but I was already complete, it was too late to say good-bye.' The communication stopped, I felt bathed in love and the golden light. I sensed that this light was Jeff and the light was in me and all things. I opened my eyes and the light show on the rock was over and it was complete."

Salt Lake City friends Jan and Magdalene told me that as soon as they heard Jeff had died they created an altar and went into meditation. Magdalene: "Jan was deeply into grief; it hit her very hard. She was identifying with what you must be going through. But my experience was very different, so different that I didn't even mention it to her: I saw Jeff sitting on a cloud, smiling broadly, full of joy."

Jeff's seventy-nine-year-old singing teacher and choirmaster in Jackson, Wyoming, felt extremely distraught upon hearing about Jeff. Then, a few days later another friend told me that Bob had had a dream in which Jeff was sitting quietly in a room—meditating, at peace—and that this dream helped Bob a great deal.

My young niece Megan found herself visited by Jeff a few days after he passed. (She had also been visited by my late sister-in-law in the same manner, calling me up to say, "Did Kathy pass? Because I think I received a visit from her.") As with Kathy, Megan did not see, but *felt* Jeff's presence "kinesthetically." At his entrance she was shocked and flustered, saying, "Oh! Are you okay?! You know you have to go towards the light!" And he answered, "Don't worry about me. I'm *fine*. Remember, I'm not a neophyte at this."

She said he told her that "there was a pipe, and that he should have been cremated with it." That "though it was just a tool, and he didn't need it where he was now, his pipe and a few other ceremonial tools need to be properly disposed of." That Megan needed to "tell Ann about this."

I knew that Jeff had been apprenticed to a Cherokee shaman for six years and initiated as a "pipe carrier," but it had not occurred to me to cremate Jeff with his pipe. How little I knew him! And how interesting that he would go to young Megan, also on a medicine path, who would understand the necessity of disposing of it properly. She and I discussed the pipe at length as well as the contents of his medicine bag; she contacted her teacher who told her to do ceremony on the medicine bag and its contents to disconnect it from Jeff and that since it was a man's pipe it needed to go to a man. We decided that she would present it to whoever would be the appropriate person. Megan then told me to wrap the contents in red cloth and ship it to her.

Jeff appeared to others as well, each time in different form, or sensed in a way appropriate to the person. For example, on the day he died, I called one of his sisters, Andrea, and was unable to reach her twin, Stephanie. Andrea called me later that evening to tell me that Stephanie was upset, because she thought she had unfinished business with her brother. Instantly I told Andrea that this was not true, that Jeff had no unfinished business with Stephanie, that he had always loved her unconditionally, that it was not in Jeff's nature to judge people. "Well then," Andrea responded, "Stephanie needs to hear that." "Tell me where she is and I'll call her," I said.

Stephanie was surprised to hear from me, and spoke in her usual cool tone. Though she graciously thanked me for talking with her I felt as if she were holding me at a distance during our phone call.

The next day Stephanie called and we spoke again. This time she was ecstatic. "Last night," she told me, "I was sitting on my bed with my cats on either side of me when Jeff appeared in a long robe." She said his presence not only freaked her out but freaked her *cats* out—(so she *knew* the experience was real).

A week after Jeff died my sister Kathy visited me from Seattle. I could sense that my attitude discombobulated her, since, to me, Jeff's "dearly departed soul" didn't seem to be "resting in peace." For from the very day he died, I had sensed Jeff as extremely active and free, joyous. Kathy would look at me strangely—until the second night of her visit. The next morning she told me that she had gotten up in the middle of the night to use the bathroom. She went back to bed, then remembered that she needed to close the door to keep the cats out. She got back up. "But when I tried to close the door, I could not. There was a strong wind blowing through the door into my face." She actually needed two hands to get that door closed. (This was a cold night in January with no windows open.)

Several days later I was looking through some of Jeff's papers, and came across an essay he wrote (the only essay that I found among his papers; he wrote reviews of and/or translated thousands of articles and books for the international journal, *Mathematical Reviews*, and for other mathematical and scientific publishers, but did very little public writing otherwise). The essay was about the Ho'oponopono ceremony, a part of the Huna religion in Hawaii. My eyes went right to a paragraph where Jeff mentions newly departed souls sometimes appearing to those left behind as a "wind."

Though both Kathy and I had instantly recognized the "wind" as a manifestation of Jeff (and its startling strength had jostled her ideas about Jeff as "resting in peace"), the fact that this interpretation was synchronously confirmed delighted me.

I am reminded of another incident that occurred the day he died. Several months earlier my friend Claudia had sent us two beautiful bowls, each painted with a different scene and in different colors, to go with the wonderful dish set she was gradually collecting for us. She thought of one of them as Jeff's and the other as mine, though she had not mentioned this.

A few hours after Jeff died, I was on the phone with Claudia when Felix jumped up on the refrigerator and then down to the counter, in the process causing something to fall to the floor and break. I walked in to see what had broken, and said, "Oh no! One of your beautiful bowls!" Instantly, she responded, "It was the green one, wasn't it." Yes. Jeff's bowl.

Jeff was manifesting on different levels and in different ways to people who each seemed to need something specific from him to communicate his entrance into the larger reality. In some cases it felt as if he and I were in cahoots, with him working on invisible planes to help me figure out how to work with a particular person's grief or their narrowly conceived views on life and what lies beyond death.

Thus he had appeared to Stephanie after I had called her, shattering her habitual reserve. And he had appeared to Kathy as a "wind," breaking into her unquestioned Catholic assumptions.

To me, he came at the Hour of the Wolf, between 2:00 and 4:00 A.M. For the first month or so, I would awaken and for those two hours be invaded with mindless agitation. Both cats also registered a disturbance in the atmosphere; they would jump up and down off my bed, and I would hear them quarreling in the living room. Only later did I realize what was going on during that nightly ordeal. The meaning came through clear contrast with what happened next.

One night I awakened as usual, this time not into an agitated, staticky void, but into what I can only describe as a warm pool of love. A love so encompassing and so thick that it seemed a kind of liquid: I felt like a baby cradled in the amniotic fluid of the womb. Or better: as though I had actually attained the blissful commingling of two souls that we women everywhere silently long for in physical lovemaking. Indeed, this sense of being enveloped in Love was so powerful and so intimate that, strangely enough—how could this be? I was alone with myself!—I actually felt somewhat "embarrassed."

Our spiritual communion lingered the entire two hours. Ever since then I feel it as the actual living space of my being when I am able to quiet myself and listen. I now sense that the agitation of those weeks during those early morning hours was caused by the attempts of our two souls to cross the barrier, to reach from our respective dimension into the other's, to carve that path between worlds. This is why I say that we now share space; in our longing for each other, we have entered the limitless void, which, paradoxically, feels utterly full.

I have one final "phenomena" story to tell that demonstrates both Jeff's continued existence and his mastery and delight in working with realms other than the one to which we are accustomed. This story concerns a friend of his, Dick, who had known Jeff since their student days as Princeton mathematicians. (Both eventually left mathematics for less abstract, more human worlds, and for nearly forty years Jeff and Dick talked regularly by phone.)

During the first few days after he died, I was determined to personally contact those who had known him best, so they would not have to hear through the grapevine. I knew Dick lived in Chicago, because Jeff had addressed a package to him the night before he died, and it still sat in front of the door. But Dick's phone was not listed in the phone book and I had not yet found Jeff's personal notebook with phone numbers in it.

Every day I would pass by the front door and wince, looking at this package, now partially buried under other packages that had come to the house since he died. (Why did Jeff order so much stuff just before he died? A new massage table, three pair of shoes, bodywork recertification, boxes of food supplements, books from England, etc., etc. I say it's because on some level, he knew he was about to leave, and another part of him wanted to anchor himself here; friends Tasha and Stephen say it's because he wanted to leave more of himself behind.) More stuff to deal with!

In my initial raw state of shock and grief, I was not capable of sitting down to handwrite a letter to Dick. I could have typed one and printed it out, but the printer wasn't working at the time. (Who was my tech support guy? Jeff!)

Finally, about ten days after Jeff died another package arrived, this one from Dick to Jeff! In a fit of frustration and pique I abruptly wrote on the package in large letters: "Deceased: Call me as soon as you get this." Such an awful way for him to hear about Jeff's death. But I was distraught, as Dick must have known when he walked in his door after being out of town to discover the box and called me, at 3:00 A.M., utterly stricken.

A few weeks later Dick called again, to say that he was "getting used to the idea of Jeff being dead, though I don't like it." And then he told me a most remarkable story.

"About five days after Jeff died (but a number of days *before* we found out about it) I woke up in the middle of the night and told my wife that I'd had a horrible nightmare, but that I couldn't remember it. Susan replied, 'I had a horrible nightmare too, and I do remember it. But I don't want to tell you.'"

But she did, and here is her dream: "Jeff Joel came to me, and said, 'I know this sounds impossible, but . . . I died. In bed, asleep, at home, of a heart attack.'" Susan couldn't believe it, and even in the dream was wrestling with the idea, thinking she had a case of mistaken identity, that maybe her ninety-year-old mentor had died. She had just spoken to Jeff three weeks earlier, and thought he would still be in Massachusetts. So it couldn't be Jeff, she thought, because he wasn't at home. And then, she told her husband, "Jeff said one more thing. He said, 'First I came back. Then I died.'" (First, he came back home, to Indiana. Then he died.)

Not only did Jeff use the dream medium to communicate his death to Dick through his wife's dream (and perhaps Dick's dream too, had he remembered it), but also, from within Susan's dream itself, Jeff was responding to her unstated doubt and confusion.

Upon hearing this and other stories, our friend Herb, who with his wife Perry had accompanied me through the entire shocky day of Jeff's early morning death—and who has long been a biblical scholar professing to be an atheist—remarked: "You are making cracks in my edifice."

"Not me." I told him. "Jeff. I am just the messenger."

Letting Go

Mid-April

"How *are* you?" Or, alternatively, "How are you *doing*?" These questions, asked with care and sensitivity and, of course, entirely well meaning, make me fidget. I feel eyes on me, scrutinizing, for any sign of—what? A sadness beyond measure? (True. But I'm not necessarily going to show my sorrow to the world.) Insanity? (About a week after Jeff died, my own sister thought I was "having a nervous breakdown," so utterly did she misread my wildly fluctuating moods.)

I remember being the one who asked such questions of others when they were undergoing a primary grief process and I was on the outside, looking in. Or trying to. Trying to show how I cared, certainly, and discretely hoping to discern, to comprehend. Unconsciously trying it out. For the day—God forbid!—when I would be on the receiving end of such scrutiny.

Mostly I fidget because I am trying not to shock people when I don't meet their expectations. So I hold myself in, and automatically put on some simulacrum of "sad" for them—an entirely different phenomenon from my private desolation.

What I must especially look out for with others who have not undergone the powerful experience of losing a beloved mate through sudden death is the leaking out of my happiness, or even, sometimes, ecstasy; so I damp myself down, to not give away this exalted sense of feeling tremendously alive. For not only would that shock them, but for me to "explain" it to them would be more than I can bear.

For what *is* true about me now is that I am hypersensitive to others, and find long conversations, and long periods in the presence of others, difficult. Exhausting. Indeed, so alive do I feel when alone, that only in others' company do I notice my current fragility.

In confronting Death, we are "reminded of our own mortality." Yes. But this may be just the surface response. For me, facing Death both stripped me of my veils and shocked me into Life.

Usually we don't have to truly face Death, this most intimate of lovers that, despite our willful ignorance of its ghostly presence, walks by our side from birth. (Or, more specifically, walks by our *left shoulder*, said shaman Don Juan to author Carlos Castaneda.) What has made *me* face Death as never before—despite my former claims of lifelong intimacy with it—is this sudden exit from the flesh of the one man who was so much a part of me that my very body cries out in anguish.

What I miss most—as any widow will tell you—is his smell. And it was my nose that—twelve years ago, during that fateful shuttle bus ride from the San Francisco airport to a conference—picked up on his olfactory signature. My nose, beyond all reason, unerringly led me to the exact person whose chemistry would activate old, ripening karma, and thereby place us on a path, together, of clearing it.

As I continue to honor the presence of Jeff's still unfamiliar absence, my relationship to Death deepens. For when Jeff died, frankly, so did I. The "I" that was the persona I presented to the world. That persona was constructed, adjusted, essentially remade, through the twelve-year friction of being faced with the continuous presence of this massive Other who had committed himself to me for good. For life! And now, I find, in death. For his death did not "do us part." His death has not severed our relationship but strengthened it. In the presence of his death, I release the persona and turn inward to the soul, its continuing relationship to his soul.

I sense that my current fragility with others stems from the lack of an appropriate persona in my interactions. Every moment feels so raw, so real. Too real, too intense for others. Every time I must say, to a grocery or bank or credit card clerk, "please take off my husband's name and replace it with mine, because he died," I must endure the discernable catch in the breath (even on the telephone!), the sudden interruption of well-oiled dailiness. Then comes the mumbled, sometimes heartfelt, usually embarrassed, condolences; and, with those to whom I must say this in person, I brace myself for the looks, the wondering, the scrutiny.

I have been having dreams of being naked in public, acutely uncomfortable. These dreams remind me of the one other time when they held this theme, and that was in my late twenties, after leaving my first marriage behind. Then, as now, I was striking out bravely, foolishly, for an unknown future. Then and now an old persona rips off. I am left naked and vulnerable, with no medium through which to encounter the world and its superficial role-playing. "Out there," I must pretend to be one thing though lacking the tools, while simultaneously working to shield the intensity of what's "in here" from view.

My friends in Jackson, Wyoming, where I lived for twenty years—Jeff moved there to be with me in 1990, six weeks after we met—cannot understand my decision to remain in Bloomington, Indiana. They were sure I would move back home. Likewise, my children assumed Jeff's death would propel me to come live with or near them in Massachusetts, and my parents and siblings in Seattle wondered if I would move there.

I read that the usual advice to those in grief is to surround oneself with loving family and friends during the bereavement process. Am I an oddball? Or am I the exception that proves that rule?

So while the hundreds of friends and family kindly leave me alone but for a few phone calls here and there, the strangers I encounter in Bloomington and by phone for one-time-only interactions involving technicalities relating to Jeff's death bear the brunt of my lack of tact, my inability to not be real, to spare them.

Actually, I must confess, there is a certain part of me that wickedly delights in the process of startling them with my announcement that, invariably, cleaves the world into before and after. I say, *my husband died in January,* and all of a sudden, for a nanosecond or two or three, the Real snaps us into its tight embrace. The air perceptibly thickens, rumbles, crackles. The disjunction between our usual sleepy half-aware state and this sudden shocking announcement from the realm of What Matters sends us reeling. How to comprehend? And more: how to fuse the seam between this collective momentary heightened aliveness and the segue back to the ordinary?

For Death is Mystery; we know essentially nothing about it while alive, though we are given tantalizing glimpses during such times as these when the veil between dimensions lifts and then, subtly, slides back in place.

Life surrounds us everywhere; the life force courses through our bodies like an inexhaustible river. The immediacy of Life is so ubiquitous that our appreciation

of its miraculous presence grows dull. The sudden insert
of Death into Life brings us up short. We are faced with
the essential mystery of our lives, the mystery we have
been forever both seeking and hiding from. Death is both
Eros and Thanatos: we lean toward it as we converge into
one lane and inch slowly by fiery highway collisions; and
we lean away from it in our daily prayers, our minute
ministrations to faces and bodies to make them appear as if
they will live forever.

Death is a study in high contrast. Death shows off
Life in all its glory. Death strips the minutiae of Life to
reveal the Soul. The contemplation of my loved one's death
throws me into ecstasy—so glad am I for him, for this
release from his physical encumbrance, this lightening of
dimensions. All of the universe opens to him. No longer is
he blinkered, caught in three dimensions and longing to be
free—meanwhile playing with musical and mathematical
harmonics, pale simulacra of what his soul sensed, in
some deep recessed place while here on Earth, as the one
fundamental song, the Music of *all* the Spheres.

And, his death left me devastated. I will never see
him in the flesh again, never smell him or feel his arms
around me, his body next to mine. My very cells long
for his comfort, the familiar security of his steady solid
presence. He was, I told him in the beginning, my battery.
All I had to do to charge myself up was to wrap myself
around him—for an hour, at first, then as the years went
on, shorter and shorter spans of time. Indeed, in the
last few years I rarely needed physical contact since our
presence together was so deeply intertwined.

But oh, at the beginning! Such sighs would erupt
from my heart during those early days of having, finally,
been found! Such primordial satisfaction, the gut knowing
that *no matter what*, he was there—here!—for me. Nothing

I could say or do would shock him into leaving—and believe me, I tested him, and he tested me, during those first few years, in ways we had never dared with others. Every time I had to tell him my truth, a truth I knew would make him furious or deeply upset, I knew he could take it, because over time he had proved that he could. He might bristle, turn abruptly, march into his room and close the door, but at some point he would re-emerge, and when he did, I would greet him with open arms and no expectations.

Not that this behavior on my part was inspired! No; it was learned, through long hard experience. At first, when I spoke my truth to him, it was not from the soul but from the persona. I was right and he was wrong and I knew how to fix him. I was the boss and he was to do my bidding. Now this attitude, of course, will never work, especially will it not work on a man with five planets in fiery, proud Leo. No matter how "true" my words, my tone was false. His response, invariably, was to stare at me with opaque leaden eyes, while retreating inside his shell. As I felt him submerge I would panic, and become even more cold and furious in my demands. From my lofty, righteous perch I judged him unmercifully for his instinctive fear of connection.

What was "wrong" was the separation between us. I intuitively knew this, and I knew that my own actions, derived from unconscious habits of a lifetime's conditioning, both helped to cause and inevitably exacerbated the distance between us. I am a fiery, dogmatic Sagittarian, and I was learning, the hard way, a more conscious approach to our issues as a couple.

Over time, I realized two things about important communication with Jeffrey.

First, I could speak my truth only once, and I was

to give it to him in a way which resonated from my soul. If I did not express myself in this authentic, vulnerable, heartfelt manner, he knew it, and by his reaction, I knew it. Thus, over time I learned, through his reflection, to discern what was really my truth and what was chatter; what was a gift from my whole being and what just steam from my talking head.

My words were a sounding from the deep. He instinctively opened to receive them. Then, given his personality's lifetime habit of total resistance to change, he would immediately close down and clam up.

I had to trust, despite his behavior, that he had heard me.

And to show my trust in him, I had to let him go. That was the second thing I learned: that each time I told my truth and we screeched to a halt, I had to, right then, internally break our connection. I had to let him go so thoroughly as to be willing for him to actually leave me. I had to jerk his cord from my solar plexus, to surrender our union so completely that, invariably, my stomach would fall through the floor. The wrench of disengagement was a plunge into the abyss.

That part never got any easier. Always, my stomach would fall through the floor. In time, my terrified response to his initial fury and disappearance signified that indeed I had spoken truth, that once again I had punctured the veneer of our social role-playing to seek the depth where the soul resides.

And if I did that, if I truly let him go each time I spoke my truth, space opened. He no longer felt cornered, and was free to be his own authentic self—and eventually, to respond. In our early years he would be gone for days, sunk in his own interior. As time went on, the lag time between call and response shortened to hours, then minutes. Each time, what that response would be, I had no idea. For in letting him go, I had to release all expectations that his response would satisfy my desires.

I had to throw the ball into his court, and then, essentially, let the whole thing go. (No obsessing on what just happened; no gloating that "I sure got to him this time." Just this, I had to concentrate on this alone: pulling out that energetic hook that bonded my solar plexus to his—while undergoing the usual painful wrench.)

By removing myself from the scene, the next step was truly up to him. And here is the most astonishing part—that response, when it finally came, would probably be from left field! And because my challenge to him to open another door always revealed him standing in a room much larger than I had imagined, I, in turn, would also be shocked into the Now. That he always surprised me with the way his essential being moved when challenged to do so was extremely stimulating.

I had told him when we married that if I ever got bored I would leave. I put him on notice that my job was to deliver shocks to his system. That because of my essentially transformative nature and path, my own spontaneous impulse would light a fire under his resistant ass, over and over again. And it did. And he was a true partner, the first man for whom I was not "too much, too intense." Time and again, as my original nature unwound around yet another new turn, Jeff's own original nature would appear out of nowhere, to meet me there. This was always surprising to one who, prior to meeting Jeff, had spent so much time "alone" (alienated) that I assumed it would be forever. In this way, over and over again, Jeffrey's unique response to my sudden call woke *me* up.

So, over the years I learned that he truly did care for me, the essential me, the one who would, at those crucial times, speak her truth, no matter how hard it was to get those words to move up from my throat where, usually, they had lodged for some time. As the years wore on, very little got stuck there. Speaking truth became easier, part of everyday life. I didn't have to pretend, or try to be better than I was, or feel guilty about anything. In his presence, nothing was forbidden and all was accepted. Our souls fit hand in glove, despite the frequent frustrating rediscovery that our personas were so very, very different—our rhythms were different, our relative needs for risk and security and for change and stasis utterly opposed.

(Adjustments to each other's styles were sometimes elaborate. For example, when we would walk in the wilderness, something we both loved to do, of course it was I who took the initiative to get him off his duff where he would invariably be reading and listening to music. Then came the elaborate preparations, which backpacks and shoes and hats, etc., and where were they? And when we finally got going, I would give him a ten-minute head start and run to catch up; that way I could take the edge off my nervous energy, and not get so annoyed and frustrated at his slow, steady pace.)

I look back now, and think, my God I really did learn how to let him go! Over and over again, with each disruption between us I breathed him out of my aura and allowed in the longing, the loss, the desolation, in order to give him room. Room to be himself, room to breathe, room to discover his own natural response.

Perhaps then, this is why my response to his death (at least so far) is not filled with what I would call "suffering." When others tell me, "Oh, this must be so hard," it's hard for me to remember to look "sad." For what I feel is puzzled at this depiction of what they think I am undergoing. Hard? No. Not really. But raw, intensely real, and still—nearly four months later—full of wild and unpredictably fluctuating moods.

Do I not suffer as expected *because* I learned to let him go in life? *Because* we practiced this surrender to the inevitable, this regular dismantling of our mutual need to control? If so, then I heartily recommend it. For no matter how much grief I encounter on my journey back into the Now, the actual process of grieving feels familiar. I know this path. This path is an old shoe. It fits my feet; it grounds me into the Real. The difference between this final letting go of his corporeal self and those other smaller letting gos along the way is that this time the process extends into the infinite. I continue to sense the endless space within which his freed being now joyfully moves, and I am presented with endless time to contemplate the ephemeral—the oh-so-precious-and-fleeting—nature of biological life.

Death closes biological life. Death is also a key that opens Life's treasure chest. Brilliant, precious, multicolored jewels spill out; they gift the senses, they nourish memory, they sooth the soul.

Our meeting and our living on this beloved Earth was transformational, rich and rare. As his life touched mine and changed me, so does his death. Life and Death chase one another in the endless spiral dance of Becoming.

Nothing is lost.

Nothing is forever.

Money and Alchemy

Late April

Given what I say about speaking truth no matter what the consequences, it may sound like Jeff and I weren't co-dependent.

Of course we were co-dependent. Not in a pernicious way, but each of us did depend on the other in certain areas of life. When we met I was forty-six years old; my rigid feminist principles had long since softened. Our division of labor tended to reflect those areas in which men and women have long felt practiced and comfortable. We didn't discuss these divisions, at least not at first, but just fell into them. Years later, each began to chafe at being taken for granted, and to ask the other to please lift some of the burden. But then, Jeff didn't live long enough for us to redistribute the weight.

Little recognitions like this one bring up short intense stabs of grief: the fact that we never got to see how we would fare in rearranging our roles! Though we had no significant emotional unfinished business, these little "what ifs," though minor, symbolize the space of endless possible transformations, now closed. Or at least closed in this earthly dimension. And today, I am not feeling the otherworldly connection that so permeated my being those first three months.

Pace feminism, our role divisions were traditional. I planned meals and cooked, he did the dishes. I was in charge of relationship atmospherics and "social life," he took care of finances and all things technical. Not that I didn't make money; there were years when I brought in more than he did. But he took charge of our physical survival and planning for security in old age. Real estate, stocks, bonds, IRAs, pension plans, mutual funds—all these accompanied him to Wyoming.

I did not even know the vocabulary of this arena, much less how to talk its language. For over a decade I had survived—and thrived!—like a gypsy. I lived in a twenty-foot-diameter yurt and rented a tiny office for astrological consultations.

I saw myself as free as a bird and him as loaded down with stuff.

He saw himself as conservative and realistic and me as irresponsible and ignorant of the world's ways.

Thus, when our relationship began, there was great disparity between us on the material plane. He was relatively "rich" and I relatively "poor," and this situational difference mirrored our personalities—indeed, I would say, was a predictable outgrowth of our personalities.

Besides having five planets in Leo, Jeff also had Moon and Jupiter conjunct in Scorpio; so he was a naturally suspicious character and had attracted experiences that, he thought, justified his paranoia. When he asked me, soon after we met, what my birthday was and I told him, the color drained from his face. "What's wrong?" I asked. "You were born the same day as Sylvia," he said, looking crestfallen. "Who's Sylvia?" I asked, curious. "She's a woman to whom I loaned $30,000 and she never paid it back," he muttered, looking embarrassed. "And she talked the same way about money that you do." Then, sneering, cynical, he mimicked her: "It'll always be there when you need it, the world is full of abundance, money is just another form of energy."

He was right, I did talk that way. This was the conclusion I had reached from *my* life experiences. As a double Sagittarian, I am naturally trusting and optimistic, and had attracted experiences that justified my light-hearted approach to the world. Specifically, my conclusion that "money is energy" had resulted from a relationship with another man, also much "richer" than I in material goods. I pause now to tell this story, since it lodged in memory as the cornerstone of my perspective on the status of "money."

Back in 1977, my monkish lifestyle was causing a crimp in my relationship with this new friend, James, a medical doctor. I was a feminist; of course I paid my own way. Our dates were limited to hikes, movies, coffee and dessert.

Finally, after a few months, James said, "Annie, we are using your survival money and my luxury money. Why not save your money for survival and just use my luxury money?" His insight, not to mention his generosity, blew me away. By reframing the subject of money, he transcended my feminist principles.

We began to do the things *he* liked to do, including fancy restaurant meals, ski vacations, and art openings in far-away cities. Of course I enjoyed the luxury and increased variety. However, I notice now in looking back, because we were using his money, he was the one who decided what we did next, and I was in the position of either delicately suggesting or waiting to find out. Had this gone on much longer, I would have begun to chafe, as I am not a natural follower.

At the time it felt good. Life was easy, and we were on easy street, having a grand time.

Meanwhile, as trust grew between us, James began to rely on me to help him investigate the significance of certain of his memories. I felt deeply familiar with this kind of project, especially when it included linking memories together to form a more conscious whole. Indeed, I had long been deeply engaged in the process of investing meaning in the entire trajectory of my life. James was a few years older than I, and just entering mid-life, the time when, as C. G. Jung noted, even normally extraverted people naturally turn inward. And though I initiated it, he was open to—even eager for—this kind of inner exploration.

I can talk about this topic now, even label it: "re-membering: putting oneself back together again." Twenty-six years ago, however, I had no perspective on my search for perspective. As a Sagittarian, my inner drive to comprehend my life as a whole felt natural and obvious. So I didn't assign what I now call "re-membering" any value, at least not consciously—as you will see when I relate what happened next.

A few months went by. Then, one evening as we were enjoying yet another expensive restaurant meal, James suddenly—out of the blue!—brought up the subject of money again. He was a sweet man, a natural diplomat, and so said, quietly and with restraint: "Annie, it's been great using my money instead of your money. We've been able to do so many fun things! . . . But it would be nice if you said 'thank you' once in a while."

Despite his mild tone, I sensed an inner intensity as he finally screwed up his courage to bring up the topic again. And I was blown away. Indeed, I felt flabbergasted, totally unhinged. This time the surprise was not pleasant and freeing, but rather, shocking and, to my mind, completely unfair.

But why was it unfair? I didn't know.

I'm sure he did not expect my shocked, hostile stare. I imagine he wished he had not brought the subject up. Yet all he was hoping for, he said, was a "thank you" once in a while. Was that so difficult?

Well, inside me a volcanic bulge was surfacing. Quickly, before it exploded on him in public, I leapt to my feet, strode out of the restaurant, and walked coatless and internally seething in thin, slick-soled boots through a howling blizzard the two miles home.

He phoned that night and the next day and for several days thereafter. Each time I would hang up on him. (This was prior to answering machines.) He came over, said he was sorry, he never should have said that. I wouldn't let him in, motioned, shaking my head "no," that he should go.

I was still terrifically upset, and still mute, completely inarticulate even to myself, as to why my feelings were running so strong and violent. I could do nothing but rage. Rage and brood, alternately. The storm within me felt so intense that I now view it as a kind of alchemy.

(I look back on that event and sense that I had plugged in to not just my own anger but into the barely submerged rage of people everywhere who have been subjected to and subjugated by our collective attitude about money. I sense that I had plunged deep into the bowels of a core contradiction within western culture, a long-term festering sore that will not heal until it is made distinctly conscious. As a child of this culture, the contradiction inhabited me too, and it was rising up, inexorably, into the light. I look back now and see this internal alchemy as not only excruciating, but utterly crucial. For as I and other pioneers mutate, so eventually, might our culture transform its terror of and preoccupation with money.)

The inner cauldron boiled on for at least a week. Finally, I began to get a handle on what was making me so angry. Why I *knew* his remark was unfair. He thought I should say thank you to him. But if that was true, I thought, then he should say thank you to me as well. While eating all those fancy dinners, our conversation had usually been centered on James; I had inspired him to consciously face up to his entire past and integrate it!

Then came an insight, bright, pure, an astonishingly simple reframing of the economics between us that placed the current disconnect and indeed our entire relationship in a new perspective. It was this: money, I realized, is *not* the "bottom line."

Here's the internal process that led to this conclusion:

I recognized that though the cliché that "money is the bottom line" is a deeply ingrained cultural assumption, it is also a manmade convention; something conjured by humans long ago. Though of course the origins of money are a matter of debate among experts and historians, in my mind I reasoned that money arose in order to facilitate generalized trading. We needed some kind of commodity that would hold its "value" beyond specific situations, and so gradually one commodity began to be valued as a "standard" that other commodities could be measured against. What that commodity was didn't matter intrinsically—cowry shells or feathers or precious metals— what mattered was its function, as "money," something with an exchange value equivalent to something else (like food, for example) that does have intrinsic value.

Therefore, I reasoned, money, since it has no value in nature, it is *not* a part of nature, *not* natural, not necessary but conventional, a form of concentrated energy that gradually emerged from the terrifically fertile human imagination as it interacted with changing experience. As a cultural trapping, money is in its essence highly abstract, not necessary but contingent; it floats on top of human nature and real human needs. Indeed, isolated pockets of "primitive" cultures may still exist that do not use "money" and whose members live richly interconnected human lives, nonetheless.

The real bottom line, I recognized from the interior of my soul after wrestling with the question for weeks, is not money but *human* energy. Each human being comes into the world with original access to a rich trove of energy and to certain talents and eventually skills that transform their unique energy into many different forms. Many years earlier I had come to terms with the fact that, given my own unique nature, my energy easily transforms into invisible forms—psychic, emotional, psychological, philosophical—and less easily into money.

Since I recognized my own natural ways of transforming energy as the foundation for what I had to offer the world, I realized this as the basis of my feeling that James's remark was unfair. *I was equal to anyone, no matter what his or her economic status.* And, of course, I gave equally in this relationship. Moreover, his relative wealth did not intimidate me, nor did it entice me. I was interested in James, the person, and I was interested in creating a relationship between us that blended our energies to transform us both.

That day I phoned James to say that I now understood what had been bothering me, and asked to see him immediately. He came right over, eager and anxious. I told him about my struggle, how I had been wrestling with the whole question of money, its place in our culture and in my life, and the need for an exchange of thank yous between us. Then I told him about my insight, that money is one way energy concentrates into form—one form of energy among others, not the bottom line; that the real bottom line is *human* energy. That, moreover, each person offers unique talents and gifts and that only some of these talents and gifts are easily translated into money.

At first he was dumbfounded, utterly stunned by this idiosyncratic way of viewing money. Then a glow spread across his face and he broke into a big smile. James's whole body visibly energized as he sensed the enormous interpersonal and cultural implications of what we both now saw as an elemental insight into the nature of money.

Our joint understanding propelled the next stage of our relationship. As James's prior reframing of money into categories had freed us to pursue our relationship in new ways, so now my reframing of our perspective on the fundamental nature of money freed us again. Soon, James bought a house for me to live in, which I then gifted to others during the daytime hours by making it the offices of *OpenSpace*, a new community magazine that I founded, and to which James contributed money. The purpose of that little tabloid magazine was to open space within our little local Idaho community, dominated by mainstream religions, for free expression of anyone who lived there.

Thus, the excruciating alchemical process within me, and the excited recognition of its significance within him, opened a space for much to happen, not only between us, but via our interactions with the world. I know this way of viewing money as "merely one energy among others, not the bottom line" may seem impossibly idealistic, even simple-minded. Nevertheless, for two years it brought about a remarkable increase in the number and variety of exchanges within one small local community and generated a great deal of excitement and good will.

So, needless to say, twenty-six years later I was more than ready for Jeff when I saw him glare at me with narrowed eyes, thinking I was another Sylvia, out to get his money through idealistic sleight-of-hand.

I did tell Jeff the story of James and me, but could feel his resistance. Hearing about another's experience meant little to him; he would have to learn from his own. Intuitively, I sensed we were in for a long period of learning trust. And I sensed that the most important quality I could cultivate within myself would be one in very short supply: patience.

As I write this, I hear Jeff intoning, in his steady, quiet manner: "Patience, Ann, patience," as he strolls into my office, having been disturbed from his reverie, in response to yet another of my strangled cries for help.

Were it not for Jeff as my "tech support guy," I would not have produced another grassroots magazine, especially one in the computer age that required me to learn Pagemaker and other technical programs. Each incomprehensible glitch brought work to a crashing halt against printer deadlines, stopping my work for the next issue of *Crone Chronicles: A Journal of Conscious Aging*, which I had founded for the free expression of a fledgling national community. And, like James before him with *OpenSpace*, Jeff contributed money to this publication that I had begun one year prior to his arrival as a tiny newsletter with $50 and a borrowed computer and that finally ended in 2001, after twelve years.

The original impasse between Jeff and myself concerning the meaning of money and its relation to human life felt very real, and seems to stem from what I would call our deepest cultural taboo. We've learned to discuss orgasms and erections, but we blush to even imagine talking about how much money we make or how much money we have.

Because it is taboo, money fascinates. We hate it and we love it. We glorify money as the source of personal worth; we're addicted to needing more and more; we despise and envy those who have more; and we tend to despise and ignore those who have less, much less, not enough even to survive. The relatively recent trend towards prenuptial agreements shows that many couples now enter marriage with an assumption that trust is naïve and divorce an expectation.

When Jeff and I first got together, my determination to learn patience was sorely tested—and not just by computers. Every day I had to witness and stop myself from judging Jeff's nickel-and-diming, of me paying for one thing, him for another, but with him reluctant, always, to show any measure of financial generosity. Once I was along when he impulsively bought not one but two sets of skiis for himself and the equipment to go with them (one of these sets sat around for so many years unused that the boots no longer fit); another day he bought a fancy mountain bike (which he used perhaps ten times in five years). He loved stuff. And he loved buying specialized equipment. Not once did he realize his stinginess toward others. He had lived as a single man for most of his life and was so self-absorbed (five planets in Leo!) that I don't think he noticed the effects of his actions on me. (Indeed, I had the distinct sense that I was the first person in his life to give him real feedback.)

He bought things for himself that I couldn't afford to buy. Not that I really wanted or needed them. What I needed was for him to notice what he was doing, the implications for our relationship, how it meant that he valued himself more than me or us.

One day, I forcefully suggested that he give all his money away. "Just give it all away," I said, dramatically. "Be like Wittgenstein. That way I would be in relationship with *you*, and not have your money come between us." Ludwig Wittgenstein was a twentieth century Austrian philosopher so riddled with guilt for having inherited money that one story, perhaps apocryphal, has him giving all his money away to a rich woman. Why a rich woman? He reasoned that since she was already corrupted his money couldn't hurt her further!

That I would pick Wittgenstein as a model is interesting as it betrays my own view of money up until Jeff's death. Smugly, and with a certain righteousness, I assumed I was free of the usual cultural assumptions about money. However, the hidden cultural idea of money as "filthy lucre" was also my own. Like Wittgenstein, I too thought money corrupted the soul. (Here's another description of the core cultural contradiction mentioned above, noted by psychoanalyst Norman O. Brown in his book, *Love's Body*: money is simultaneously both slimy shit and glittery gold.)

Well, you can imagine how I upset this imperial Leo when I suggested, even demanded, that he give away all his money!

However, it was soon after that his attitude toward me softened. Less and less did he compare me to Sylvia. He still didn't trust me completely—because "Who knows," I can imagine him thinking, "women know how to seduce men in ways that men don't even realize"—and it's true, I admit I did seduce him that way.

At the time, my demand that Jeff give away all his money was accompanied by romantic images of the two of us, unburdened by any prior attachments, working hard to survive and thrive, while deepening intimacy as we forged a life in common. In hindsight, however, I realize that asking him to give away all his money because I wanted to be in relationship with him and not have his money stand between us was perhaps the strongest possible way for me to let him know my real intentions. I did want to be with *him*. I was *not* with him for his money.

So he did begin to relax a bit, and over time learned to trust that the man I loved was not the rich man but the inner man. However, to the day he died Jeff was in charge of our finances. Partly because he was used to it and I was glad not to have to deal with it: but mostly because he still liked that kind of "control" and I still thought of money as "dirty." I am sad to say (another missed opportunity) that we never did penetrate through the taboos around Money, this most sacred/profane talisman in our profoundly materialistic culture.

So, when he died, this was obviously one area that had me absolutely panicked. How would I do it? How would I even understand it? That First Night, the shock of his death not only left me psychically suspended between heaven and earth, it also ignited my terror of having to learn the language of finances, to take charge of an alien earthly realm that I both feared and hated. And yet, of course, as much as I felt afraid of being corrupted, I was also secretly excited about the freedom, the opportunity and the challenge his money presented—and then felt guilty for feeling that. How callous! Didn't I love him? Did I want him dead?

So many times Jeff had muttered, with a Scorpionic sting, "I'm worth more to you dead than alive." And that remark had always made me flinch. But why? Because I wanted him alive? Or because I was afraid of what would happen if he died? Or both? I think both.

I liken my fear of money to my fear of mathematics

that began in first grade, when during an arithmetic lesson I blurted out the question, "What is a number?" No doubt Sister Mary Bernita was taken by surprise, and while trying to think up an answer she silently stared at me so long and hard that everyone turned to look and my ears burned. Finally, she said, "That is not a question, dear." From that moment on, math was a floating world, with no obvious anchors in reality.

So too here. Jeff's death dropped me into a floating pool of relative wealth, with no obvious anchors to my former reality. The disjunction between my previous self-image as a gypsy outside the mainstream and my instant cultural status as a "rich man's widow" threw me into deep inner turmoil. The fire has been lit under another alchemical cauldron, and still boils away. At some point I hope to understand and act upon the mutation caused by this transformation of my personal and cultural identity.

For nearly a quarter of a century I have been fascinated with the phenomenon of money: its origin, the uses to which it is put, its relationship to social roles and psychological states, its paradoxical function as a sacred taboo. Now I have been gifted with a legacy that feels like a treasure chest, at once albatross and sacred trust. I can hear Jeff's deep, guttural laugh as he looks on me and my predicament: "Okay, ma'am (why did he used to call me "ma'am"?), *now* what are you going to do? How will you put *my* money where your mouth has been all along?"

Yes, how am I to steward this extraordinary opportunity his death handed me?

As Jeff anchored me in life, so his legacy anchors me in death. I need this anchor, I realize, to ground and balance my own flighty nature. What kind of an anchor I choose it to be is yet unknown. I await the outcome of the current alchemical process.

The Lawnmower

Early May

Back in 1966 I was a first-year doctoral student in philosophy, with one of the requirements a graduate course in "Logic." The material was easy to learn and seemed quite "logical;" however, I experienced an interesting, bifurcated reaction. My mind was bored, but my body squirmed as if held in a closely confined space.

Finally, near the end of the first semester, I suddenly interrupted the professor's presentation to ask, in all innocence: "But what's *wrong* with contradiction?"

Well, judging by the look on his face, that was not a normal question. Indeed, the professor seemed so flustered, and his face so full and red, it seemed ready to burst! Again, there was that same staring as in first grade, although this time I did, finally, get an answer. Shaking his head in dismay, the professor sputtered, "Because from a contradiction, anything follows! *Anything*!"

At the time I was puzzled by his response and mortified by the sudden frisson it caused in the class. In retrospect, I feel for the professor, and understand how our brief interchange caused a sudden shattering of classroom decorum.

Logic functions as a set of rules for "deriving" sentences from one another so that the "truth-value" remains the same from beginning to end. If the assumptions of any particular logical chain are "true," and if the interim steps are carried out according to logical rules, then the conclusion will be guaranteed "true." I like to think of logic as a set of pipes that moves "truth" from one place to another.

Thus, logic is a linear process; in a "logical argument," sentences "follow" one another in a straight line. There are no analogical asides, no charms or incantations, no spacious fuzzy descriptions, no colorful metaphors or juxtaposed synchronicities, no word plays or puns, no rhythm or tone, no grand overarching conclusion sweeping all before into one thundering symphonic chord. All these "soft," "fanciful" attributes are the province of what we now call (fuzzy) "right-brain" thinking, as opposed to "hard"-wired logic's "left-brain" imprimatur.

The idea of a functional distinction between the two halves of the brain had not yet entered the vernacular in 1966. In fact, soon after the disturbing event in Logic class, I was excited to read an article in the current issue of *Scientific American* which posited that the brain's left and right sides harbor distinctly different modes of thought. (My memory of this moment segues into another from a year earlier: sitting in rapt attention as C. P. Snow talks about his new book *The Two Cultures* [of Science and Art].)

I was twenty-three years old in 1966, and very much conditioned by my regular schooling and what is still a profound and little noticed cultural bias for what we have collectively learned to call "left-brain thinking." But here I was, for the second time in my life, asking a question that couldn't be answered from within the framework of the subject being studied. Just as "What is a number?" takes one out of mathematics into philosophy, so does my question about contradiction, and especially his answer to my question, imply that there may be mental worlds larger than the one inhabited by linear strings of thought.

Contradiction, in logic, functions as a wall, "that beyond which one dare not go." The wall is both formidable and so ubiquitous as to go unnoticed. My professor was clearly both flabbergasted that I would dare question the immutable role of contradiction and frightened by the implications of his own answer. For if anything follows, then—then what? What happens to standards, boundaries, structure, rules? Indeed, what happens to right and wrong? Are there no limits? Or are we condemned to a "relativism" that justifies anything and everything, a Hobbesian nightmare of anarchy and chaos that will dismantle the entire painstakingly built edifice of western civilization?

I have been wrestling with just these questions ever since. And no, I don't think the consequences of including the logical function of contradiction in a larger field of exploration need be all that dire.

I feel at home in the more spacious world of "right-brain" intelligence. Meanwhile, however, I still have to live in "the (left-brain) world" as currently constructed, from which Jeff, when he was alive, shielded me. Jeff was a vast being, comfortable in both worlds of science and art, technique and magic, logic and poetry. No realm of mental and spiritual exploration was foreign to him.

In the last chapter I spoke of my fear of working with finances, and akin to this is my fear of anything involving machines, including computers. Now, since I found that Logic course easy, one would think that working with machines would also be easy for me. Again, I have a block—probably more emotional than intellectual—but very, very real. Years ago, while living alone, I would wait until my friend Ellen came over and then ask her to figure out what was wrong with my vacuum cleaner, or how to hang a curtain, or even put up a nail for a picture on the wall. After Jeff died, Ellen came to Bloomington to visit, and once again I had a list of technical jobs waiting for her: hang a new curtain, change the message on the answering machine, reset a digital clock.

This is all leading up to a banner day in my post-Jeff era—the day when I figured out what was wrong with the lawnmower—another of the "little things" that, when first encountered, tend to overwhelm me. I am happy to report that I am now master of my lawnmower.

I had been thinking about the fact that I needed to get the lawnmower out of the basement and get it ready—check the oil, get new gas—since the first flush of spring green in mid-March. Yet every time the problem of that lawnmower lurking down there appeared in my mind's eye I immediately banished it as too thorny to contemplate. After all, I had Death on my mind! And it was true: I did need to let the small things go while I worked to incorporate this life-transforming event.

But of course, the business of the lawnmower was inextricably linked to his death, part of the needed transformation. Jeff had been in charge of the lawnmower, and so his death thrust its care completely on me, a neophyte with no desire to learn.

As with other such tasks, such "small things," I was giving myself time to recover from my great loss and pushing intruding thoughts aside. They made me stiffen in fear, or annoyance. "Who needs that?" I would think. Instead, whenever I found myself obsessing on such things as lawnmowers I would run yet another hot bath into which I would pour a lavish amount of scented bath salts. I knew it was important to treat myself to little luxuries during this unprecedented difficult time. Warm water was one substitute for the warmth and comfort of his body (the cats help now, especially Selena, my "lap kitty"). My body relished the hours in the tub, and I felt grateful to myself for this nightly gift. Indeed, I went so far into the luxury of hot water that I allowed myself not only that bath before bed, but a hot shower in the morning as well.

Four days ago, I decided I could wait no longer. I simply *had* to get up the courage to tackle the lawnmower project. The grass was growing like crazy, and rain threatened for the next few days. Putting it off would make mowing later more difficult. I had only that day's window of time.

Thus prodded to get going, I determinedly marched down the stairs and into the basement room where the lawnmower hunkered, right where Jeff had stored it for the winter.

While I had sort of prepared myself for the oil and gas business, the first hurdle was completely unexpected: how to get it through the basement door and negotiate the sharp right turn up the outside stairs?

The lawnmower just wouldn't make that turn. No matter how I tried to corner it, tip it one way and then another, it refused to squeeze out the door, turn on the landing and then up the stairs. How could this be? It got down the stairs and into the basement, so surely it could also go up. And it had to, it simply had to! The lawnmower was too heavy to lift; I couldn't just carry it up sideways but had to bump it up the stairs on its wheels.

As usual, in my frustration with machines, when one way didn't work, I tried it again, the same way—and of course got the same result, which drove me absolutely crazy. I was burning with fury at this damn thing, which had me flummoxed even before I got it outside.

This was the time when I would have screamed, "Jeffffffff!!!" or, pre-Jeff, would have waited for Ellen.

But one of my rescuers was dead and the other a thousand miles away. I could have alerted a neighbor—I have become acquainted with several who are kind and probably willing—but something in me knew this was a watershed moment. *I needed to change this lifelong habit of calling for help instantly with any frustration over a machine.* Furthermore, as one computer expert explained to me: "If one way doesn't work, try another way! Machines are logical. They are not mysterious!"

I told myself these things, the same things Jeff would tell me, and this time I had to hear them. Jeff's death had reverberated into all the interstices of my nervous, restless habits. I was determined to uncover my original self underneath those encrustations, and I knew, with every fiber of my being, that there was some part of me that, once uncovered, would and could competently deal with this situation. I knew that I was faced with another emotional block, not a real problem.

Finally I stilled the internal chaos triggered by frustration and managed to focus my eyes on the actual machine. I told my eyes to slow down and travel over every single part of the lawn mower, to see if another idea would come to me.

Hmmm. Maybe the handles fold?

Eureka! They do!

That was my first success in an afternoon filled with seemingly intractable problems.

The next step was to go buy "new" gas. There was a tiny bit of gas in the can from last fall, but that was "old," so I figured I needed to get rid of it, and maybe they would have a place to dump it at the gas station. I carefully placed the can on the floor of the car and drove to a nearby gas station, where, of course, they *didn't* have a place to dump it! "Then what shall I do?"—a question that, since his death, flows from my mouth like water, and invariably, people are kind and helpful. (Are they kind because, since his death, I look at once so stupid, so vulnerable, and so willing? Or is it because I am now living in the Midwest, and it truly *is* the "heartland"?)

The gas station attendant prefaced his advice with the usual words, "Well, what *I* would do is . . . go home and pour it out in my driveway."

So I got back in the car and drove home and trickled the "old" gas onto the driveway, then drove back and filled the can with "new" gas.

I was feeling pretty good by this time. The hassle of getting gas was over. It felt like I was halfway there. Little did I know, but my time with the lawnmower was just getting started.

Next, the instruction booklet told me to check the oil. It was slightly down, so I filled it with the oil I found near the lawnmower's original basement position, guessing that Jeff must have put it there after filling it (and hoping it was the right oil). I have to be careful: "Caution, do not overfill."

It's hard for me to absorb the information. My eyes tend to bounce off the page. Okay. Sit down. Relax. Have a cup of tea and re-read the instructions.

Okay. Done. I cannot put it off any longer. Now I have to get down to the real business and I think I know the steps to follow. Sigh. Time to actually start the machine. First I must hook up the spark plug. Moment of panic. Where is the spark plug? What does a spark plug look like, and is it obviously visible? Ah yes, there it is, in front, plain as day, and there's the cap to snap onto it, too. Done.

Then I must prime the primer three times. Primer?!? Ah yes, the red pillow-like button, near the spark plug. I push the primer in with my finger, slowly and deliberately. One. Two. Three.

Okay, the moment of truth. I walk around to the back, hold the "control bar" down with one hand while pulling out the "starter handle" with the other. Nothing.

Sinking feeling.

Pull it out again. Nothing. And again. And again. Nothing! Panic starts in my stomach, an acrid taste bubbling up my throat.

There's that urge to scream for help, to scream "Jeff, *Jeff*!"

I don't scream, and the silence of his not being there to answer hits me like a cannon ball. The world drains of color as I double up in pain with the usual, periodic— triggered by incidents like this one—desolation.

But I have been undergoing this same process, triggered by one tiny thing after another into deep spasms of grief, since early January. It is now early May. By this time another part of me is quite aware of both my panic and my urge to scream. Standing here in back of the lawnmower with my hands on the controls in the middle of a beautiful soft green flowering Indiana spring day, it is as if time has slowed down and I am watching myself in a film, experienced as a sequence of stop frames. Along with the acid bubbling up, is an unmistakable seed of humor. I am taking a wry look at myself, now that this exact situation I had dreaded most, the one I obsessively imagined every time I postponed this task, has come true.

Okay. Where am I? Oh yes, trying to get the lawnmower to start. Maybe I flooded it. Give it a few minutes. I walk in the house with head down, dejected. But my mind is buzzing: "Okay, maybe I should call Sears, where we bought the damn thing last August. No, maybe I should just go over there, it isn't very far. Should I take the lawnmower with me? No. I can't lift the damn thing."

Once I get in the house my body heads straight for the phone and, after figuring out where "Sears" would be in the yellow pages (that took awhile) I found myself talking with someone in the Lawn and Garden department.

With great authority, he tells me there are only two things it could be. One: it needs a new spark plug. Or, two: there's "bad gas" in the carburetor. I told him I didn't think that was it because my husband had run the machine until it ran out of gas, as per the instruction booklet, before putting it away. And, how could it need a new spark plug already, when the machine had only been used a few times? The desperate wavering voice probably alerted him to my nervous, unstable, wits-end condition. He then said, in a comforting tone, "Want to bring it in?" At which point I almost sobbed that it was too heavy to lift.

I ended up driving over there (sans machine) and spoke to yet another man, who told me the same thing (thank God for small favors!), but did so in a slow, kindly midwestern manner. In fact, his physical presence was so reassuring that I felt free to ask questions, wondering what "bad gas" is and what to do about it, how to unplug a spark plug and how to know if it needed to be replaced, etc. He responded to all my questions thoroughly and by the time we were finished I felt a lot better.

(Now, if I could just keep all this new information in my head! One of the symptoms of grief is that my memory is even worse than usual. But maybe this forgetting is one of grief's gifts, plunking me down into the present moment over and over again.)

I told him I wanted to buy a spark plug, just in case it wasn't "bad gas." My new friend praised me for covering all the bases. I swelled with pride.

And, of course, lawnmower sparkplugs have to

have a special kind of sparkplug wrench, so he handed me one of those too. And just in case I couldn't figure out how to use the wrench when I got home, I asked him if I could take the sparkplug out of the plastic casing and fit the wrench onto it. (Really silly of me, as it was obvious at first glance how it worked. But at this point I needed to give myself all opportunities to let go of panic, and knew that if I tried it before I left the store, I might be able to do it at home and avoid the habitual internal disconnect.) He was very obliging, and if he felt I was stupid, didn't show it.

I think it was at about this point when I made the announcement, sure to change everything: "My husband died recently, and so this is all new," etc., etc. I am shameless; I will use Jeff's death whenever it promises to ease my way. And it always does. (How long will I keep this up before I *do* feel ashamed? Just when do I no longer count as a "new widow"?)

So, clutching the bag with my two small purchases I exit Sears and drive home. I walk to the back patio where the malevolent creature still hunkers, mocking me. But at this point there is a little spring in my step. In fact, I am sort of marching over to the lawnmower, as if I know what I'm doing. As if I can get myself to think that and the lawnmower will cower and obey.

I get out the wrench and place it around the machine's spark plug as instructed, hoping I can get it to turn (worried that I can't). Ah! Yes! This marvelous tool is exactly built to exert the leverage needed. Now I am appreciating a real-world tool! This is a brand new experience. I have never before consciously honored the form of a tool as perfectly and economically designed to fulfill its specific function.

When the spark plug finally comes out I turn it upside down to look to see if it is "blackened," as instructed. Ah! Yes, again! So glad I got the spark plug, even though the clerk had thought "bad gas" the more likely problem. How prescient of me! Now I am appreciating myself! Another new experience in this kind of situation.

I replace the old sparkplug with dispatch. Looking at me screw that new sparkplug in, you'd think I'd used that wrench a million times, so expert and confident did my behavior appear.

Okay, the problem was the spark plug. Now it should start. . . .

Wrong. (Silent gnashing of teeth.)

Don't give up! Try again, and remember, the man said that if at first, it doesn't start, prime it again. That the function of the primer is to push the "new" gas into the carburetor so that eventually it will dilute the tiny amount of "old" gas still in there. Push it more than three times, push it five times. Or even ten! Just keep priming and trying to start. Eventually the machine will take off. If you think you might have flooded it, then wait ten minutes, before priming and trying to start again.

And that is exactly what I did. The process took about fifteen multi-pull tries, each time priming five to ten times. Of course I got discouraged, and wondered if it wasn't going to work after all. At one point I thought I might have flooded it, and decided to take a break for tea. I walked into the house so filled with discouragement that it was one of the blackest moments in these four months since Jeff died. I did almost give up. But then, when I walked out to the backyard again, primed it five times and pulled out the starter handle, the lawnmower unexpectedly roared into life! The joy and exultation of that moment more than balanced my previous despair.

I zipped around front and back yards in that same

exultant state, thrilled with the noxious fumes, loving the vibration against my hands. Like a animal marking its territory, I was traveling over all the humps and patches, digging into the far corners, sidling up to and around trees, stomping on all the weird grassless mounds left by those pesky voles (or are they moles?).

I did it!

One down.

Many more to go. There's the scanner to connect to the computer and learn how to use. There's the fax and copy machines to set up. There's my email, which keeps glitching. There's the new phone to replace the old one and the clogged drains on the roof. What tasks can I learn to do myself and what to give to service people?

Jeff! *Jeff*! I hear the screaming in my head, but it is a fading echo. I smile at this silliness which still grabs me and shakes me loose from former fears. I should be grateful that such "real world" stuff slows me down. Grateful for material reality so dense and thick and riddled with things that go "wrong." Given all these responsibilities, there's no way I can join Jeff at this point, nor would I want to.

Yes, I *am* grateful to be no longer suspended between Heaven and Earth, glad to be one of Earth's all-too-human inhabitants.

Basking in the present moment, left-brain slowly winking on, I await with a tiny shiver of pleasure *whatever* comes next.

$\mathcal{A}$ Gift in the Proximity of Death

Mid-May

   "Grief is another country," I emailed to someone a few days after Jeff died. And I'm still traveling through that country, over four months later.

   This new landscape feels huge. I've only begun to explore it and its changing weather, my moods; they pass through like breezes on a summer day. The geography varies greatly: there is the city, and its labyrinthian bureaucracies that I must negotiate to prove my husband has died and I am his widow; there are the small towns, where the mailman, the handyman and the UPS man all know my name and I know theirs, where I feel supported by a silent but gracious network of family, neighbors, new and old friends; there is the desert—long, flat places where not much happens in the busy day and I savor secret solitary journeys to the stars at night; there are the jagged mountains—dizzying heights and chasms that my body craves and whose winding rocky paths it is in fine shape to walk up and down. (I thank the Goddess for my physically fit body as I entered this process, and that I have retained my morning tai chi practice; I sense that were my body not strong, I would not be able to channel the turbulent emotions without breakdown.) And finally, there are cool green shady forests, where I sometimes feel grateful to get lost for days, and where I can lie down for a nap, to rest up for the next swift river I fear crossing.

Throughout this journey, for me, a big question: some of what I am undergoing feels so cataclysmic and seismic that I wonder if it really belongs to me. What is my personal grief and what is not? And, what *is* this other?

Despite my current preoccupation with exploring this unknown country, there are times when I am whisked back into my old familiar pre-death landscape, and during those minutes or hours or even days it is as if grief does not exist, as if the fact of Jeff being present or absent has no bearing whatsoever on my well-being. Then, often as not, I feel guilty: that I don't honor his death enough; that I am a cavalier person who dismisses loved ones with a wave of the hand.

But that's absurd, for my life *did* cleave in two on that fateful morning when I found his body lying still and silent on the bed. There is that "before" life and there is this "after" life, or better, *afterlife*. For it is indeed true: what I have described as being suspended between Heaven and Earth can also be described as being suspended between Life and Death. For a while both were equally real, held equal value. Indeed, as I recounted in "Phenomena," for the first few months I could not separate the two; they swirled together in a mist that spilled in all directions and dissolved horizons.

There were times, and I just now admit this to myself, when "I" felt so unreal, so little a part of life on earth, that I longed for cessation of struggle. I yearned to ignore this "opening of the eyes" to the *real world* that has been the startling accompaniment of grief, and seemingly in direct opposition to it. Grief seeks to descend, to "curl up and die," to simply vanish, and never be seen again. Grief sees no advantage in life, or, I should say, no more advantage in life than in "death"—whatever *that* is: thus the sense of being suspended.

And yes, I admit to myself now, on occasion I did briefly tip over the edge internally, and wish to be whisked off this world to join him in his mysterious otherland. Should I call this wish "suicidal"? Should it have worried me or anyone else? I don't think so. I would rather call it a bending of the soul to the Other whose absence envelops one like a shroud, and I would be more concerned if a person undergoing such a primary grief process did *not* long at times to join the netherworld of the beloved.

As this process wears on what I notice now is the relativity in my experience of time. Sometimes the alternations between yes and no, life and death, are so rapid that it feels both are true at once; at other times it is as if I am drifting on a sea of long slow swelling life which then turns and flows into death's troughs, equally long and slow. This strong but equal ambivalence is, actually, now that I think about it, not new to me; and perhaps the following story is worth telling.

The one other time I experienced the strange but harmonious duet that holds life and death in the balance (and both in abeyance) took place on a late February afternoon in 1976 in southern Idaho. I was with two men: Joe, in his early twenties; and Dennis, in his late thirties—and, salient fact, given what happened next—we were stoned on magic mushrooms.

The men were in a macho mood, something not characteristic of either of them. Perhaps it was the chemistry between them, or perhaps they wanted to show off for me, I don't know, but in any case, at one point the older man, Dennis, threw down a gauntlet. "We're going to get Dan's canoe and go down the river!" he proclaimed with great fanfare. And of course Joe and I, drunk on beauty too, couldn't wait to encounter the canyon's narrow crevasse and the Snake River's sinuous curves.

That was about 2 P.M. By the time we got the canoe loaded on its trailer and hooked up to Dennis's Jeep, dropped Joe's car at the take-out spot, drove to the put-in, smoked a joint, unloaded the canoe in the water, donned heavy jackets, gloves, hats and scarves, another hour and a half had gone by. Despite the group euphoria, my little ticker was busy counting. The sun would set around 5:30 P.M. and go behind the canyon walls about an hour earlier. We had only five miles to go on the water, but the river was slow. Would we make it out by dark?

Something in me was gearing up for trouble, and my conscious mind identified it as having to negotiate the dark in a flimsy canoe while on mushrooms. Just as we were about to enter the canoe, I said to Dennis, my voice betraying anxiety, "Do you think this is a good idea?" He, of course, dismissed my question with a laugh.

Thus cowed into submission—I was, at that point in my life, still prone to put others' wishes ahead of my own—I committed myself to the journey. Despite my better judgment, my unconscious screaming "*No!*" I gingerly placed my right booted foot into the stern of the canoe and then my left. Joe did the same in the bow of the canoe, and Dennis then heaved his bulk into the middle and shoved off. Note that this was normally a two-person canoe; the weight of the three of us brought the water to within a few inches of the canoe's rim.

But never mind. We were high on life, and we were going to have a glorious time.

By this time I had rationalized my fear, thinking it a replay of my old childhood fear of anything new, especially if it involved pitting my physical self against unknown dangers in the wild. Furthermore, I was in an interesting transition, having just divorced the man who had been the love of my life as a teenager, and whom I had finally married in my early thirties. The marriage had lasted only as long as our mutual need to heal our broken "first-love" union, and to indulge our sexual heat twelve years after chaste Catholic beginnings.

For almost exactly one year we enjoyed near-continuous lovemaking. Then, suddenly, one morning I no longer wanted to make love. I felt sated with love's sweetness and now a decidedly different desire had reared its troublesome head. From that day on, I was driven to understand. What lay beneath? How, if at all, were our natures configured together?

Dick and I had been enacting the emotional/physical bond that had drawn us together as teenagers. But we were no longer just smitten kids, we were adults with lives and paths that may or may not converge. That morning's awakening led to another year of passion: marathon daily discussions of what we gradually came to realize as divergent goals, lifestyles and philosophies. His job as editor of our home-town newspaper was the big issue; it required his spouse to play a certain role as his helpmeet and social director. Was I capable of doing this? Was I even vaguely interested? (No.) Turning the tables, would he be willing to leave his job, to begin another publication, with me as his partner? (No!)

As the year wore on, I began to reluctantly accept that Dick was happy in his work and that I was not willing to adjust to his life. Mainly because, as his "wife," I couldn't do my work. "But what is your work?" Dick would ask plaintively, wanting to be patient, and yet beginning to realize that I might actually leave him despite our fairytale love. "I have no idea!" I would answer. And I didn't. All I knew was that remaining by his side would inhibit the unfolding of my own nature.

This discovery felt terrible, for it meant that I

would have to forego the security and sense of trust and happiness that I had finally found after so many years of dreaming of Dick while in the arms of someone else. Dick was and is a truly wonderful man, and our physical and emotional compatibility was solid and real. Leaving him was inconceivable to my "logical" mind, but necessary to that greater mind that knew better what was in store for me and was determined to follow that destiny.

Thus did our dream-come-true ultimately, and reluctantly for us both, transform into a bubble—that burst. After only two years of wedded bliss, Dick gently and with great care set me free to follow my path, whatever it was. At first, in a tiny studio apartment and with no clear goal or means of support, I found myself in shock at my own decision, and, of course, wondered, was I a fool? Wavering. Should I go back?

There's nothing like danger to concentrate the mind, to propel oneself forward on the exact course that is right for the Self. So, six weeks later, my unconscious arranged for me to find myself this canoe with two men, one older, one younger. . . .

And my premonition proved correct.

At first, all was as we had imagined. On both sides, deep dark angular volcanic rock cliffs laced with ice-crystal waterfalls glinted in late afternoon sun. Above, clear blue sky; below, smooth green water slowly curved through canyon walls, framed in beige and grayish green grasses, a few stark trees and sage.

Silence. Only the rippling of oars through water. In the back and unseen by my companions, I struggle with fear and foreboding. Castigating myself for ruining my own good time. Every few minutes I silently calculate just where we are on the river, our progress from put-in to take-out. My chief fear is that we will not make it out by dark, for the river runs just as slow as I had feared.

But never mind. Listen! What's that whirring noise ahead? Ah! We all gasp as the beating of a thousand duck wings fan upwards at our approach. Several times we are immersed in this unearthly sound, as the ducks circle and again descend to the river ahead. This extraordinary and unexpected treat plunks me right out of my mind and into the present moment.

And ah! What is *that*?! A different sound ahead, a sort of rushing white noise. Since this is my first "river trip" I have no associations with this sound. Twenty-six years later, having been on several week-long river trips and one glorious three-week trip down the Colorado in the Grand Canyon, I know very well what that hissing noise means: rapids. At the very least an interruption in this slow meandering, and an opportunity to practice alertness. Rapids to negotiate. Rapids to negotiate in an overloaded canoe.

I had been sitting there thinking maybe we would make it after all, that my fears were unwarranted. At this point, I calculated that we were about halfway. I could already just make out the road ribboning down the canyon to the take-out point, and assumed the point itself would soon be visible.

As we made the turn in the river we entered the "rapids," what I have learned since to classify as "Class 1"—hardly anything, more a long series of strong ripples. But our overloaded canoe could easily tip. The men were overjoyed at this test of their prowess, which didn't reassure me at all. Silently, this skeptic in the back seat closed her eyes and thought: "What will get me through is grace and balance, grace and balance. Just hold tight and center myself in the exact middle of the canoe."

Amazing. It worked! We were all thrilled to still be

upright after this riffle rounding the river's curve which at times brought the water within an inch of the rim. Ah! I thought to myself, so that was it, the danger I sensed, now passed.

Not so fast. The men were now segueing from excitement to a swollen, prideful state. Both of them, really expanded. Suddenly one pointed to a little curtain of water falling about three feet into the river. "Hey, let's go up that waterfall!" he said, and the other instantly agreed. "Yeah!" And they began to madly paddle back upstream, to where the waterfall's current entered at a nearly right angle to the main current.

What? Such foolishness! I knew we couldn't go up that waterfall, that this was the mushrooms talking. Sudden sinking into pit of stomach as I passively endured the approach to what was fated to become one of Life's great Initiations.

When the canoe hit the waterfall current it whipped it around and one side tipped to the point where the canoe started to take on water. Then, abruptly, we were all in the river and another dream had come true.

I remember coming up from below with an absurd thought: "Where is the *deus ex machina*? Okay, the fun's over, we've learned our lesson. Now pluck us out of the here!" I demanded of what should have been a giant unseen hand.

Nope. The waterfall current was sweeping us into the middle of the river, as fully dressed, booted, and waterlogged (the men both startled and sheepish) we all clung to the overturned canoe: Joe at the bow, Dennis at the stern, and me in the middle.

We drifted this way for several stunned minutes, the men trying to remember from Boy Scout days how to right an upside-down canoe, arguing back and forth, trying out

the stars know what is
in the ocean, and the fish
becomes a mouth devouring
the thistles on the heath.
why don't you come back
inside before you freeze?
I'm here because
the only thing left for me
is death.

(11. IX. 1969. 0305)

Left page: Jeff in his childhood
Upper right page: Jeff's maternal grandmother
Lower right page: Jeff with his mother

CRANE SBILL (Geranium robertson
Geranium family
major-league
astringent . Strongest ROOT
astringent. easily available here
(Bistort in high meadows)
(only other plant is Stinkwort)
In dry areas more numerous
useful 1st aid dusting powder :
astringent (especially one that has

-8-

AND GO, AS LOW AS YOU
CAN / EXPENDED —
INTERNALIZING THE
SOUND
THESE ARE PRIMAL
PRE-LANGUAGE SOUND
HEALING IS NOT IN GOD
— NOT THIS & NOT THAT
IT IS THE RELATION BETWEEN
THEM.
THINK OF THE MOVEMENT
RATHER THAN THE OBJECT
① ADD MOVEMENT. HOLD
ANKLE (PART OF LEG) WITH HAND
ALLOW LEG TO MOVE WHERE IT
WILL. CIRCULAR, FLOW. NOT
DIRECTED.

-7-

IF WE KEEP LOCALIZING
OURSELVES (WITHOUT AWARE-
NESS OF IT), WE
RESTRICT OURSELVES / THE
AMOUNT OF INFO. AVAILABLE
TO US.
"WHAT ARE YOU
FEELING NOW?" IS A
LOCALIZING QUESTION.
UNWINDING OF SPINE
↑ REFINING MOVEMENT
THRU SOUND
INNOVATE — CREATE IN
NEW ORDER OF HUMAN
② EXPAND FLOATING / DROPPING
HEAD TO TO SH . ALLOW
SELF TO COME FORWARD INTO FORM
THE THRUST FOR LIFE IS IN TUSH

anaerobe
Gram +

— root for tea —

dry & grind together in a powder

Can add :
/ Cicatria Mtn. Hollyhock or Mallow leaves
Blither
1/2 with mixture. Can make a poultice
too

My friend Kate took this photo after a Dances of Universal Peace weekend in early December, 2001.
She didn't send it to me until after he died, 13 months later because, she said, "the look on his face told
me that he was done with this world, ready to die." In the picture I appear oblivious

different alternatives. Nothing worked.

Time had slowed to a crawl. I was in the middle, in more ways than one. In a flash, my life up to this point passed before me as I asked myself: "Do I have any regrets? Is there any choice I would have made differently?" And the answer was no. All was as it should be. It was at this point that I entered a transcendent zone that I recognize once again, twenty-six years later, during my mourning process in early 2003. A sense that either alternative, Death or Life, was fine. That there was no felt difference between the two, they swirled together in one timeless unity. My larger being included both as options so that which one prevailed truly didn't matter.

Needless to say, we did manage to exit the river, just as dusk fell. That evening we sat around for hours to hash through our ordeal, and discovered vast differences in our experiences.

For Joe, in his early twenties, the dominant thought was that this stupid river was not going to defeat him. He was too young to die and would succeed in making it to shore, no matter what the odds!

For Dennis, in his late thirties, and a pathologist who knew the amount of time a human body could spend in a near-freezing river and live—eight to ten minutes— we were sunk. There was no way we were going to get out of that river. But he did not let his pessimism show, and throughout the ordeal pretended to be upbeat and encouraging.

And then there was me, dreamily poised to go either way.

Finally, after what seemed an eternity, Joe had said, "To hell with the canoe! Let's swim for it!" Trust the young one whose survival instinct ran strong enough to realize that what was keeping us from escaping the river was our need to be responsible for the borrowed canoe! We yanked off our boots, released the canoe to its fate, and headed for shore. (The next day we found the canoe downriver, stranded on rocks.)

That event seared into memory. Whenever I doubted myself, I would recall my serene sureness in that river: that all my major decisions in life, so far, had been correct, that there was nothing to regret. The propulsion from that one event was good for decades of new choices.

And now the initial shocky phase of my mourning from Jeff's sudden death produced the same response within me.

It appears that the immediate felt proximity to death, when acknowledged and embraced, opens the door to a wider perception. Interestingly enough, this opening also ushers in a mysterious sense of safety and security that has nothing in common with any mechanical *deus ex machina* but seems more akin to the feeling of an infant held in her loving mother's arms.

I had lost the security of Dick's arms, but I had been found by the universe. From that time on, no matter how deep my absorption in petty concerns, another part of me can, when called upon, re-enter that feeling of spaciousness, that warmth in the middle of a cold dark river. In the same way, when Jeff died, leaving me alone in a little house in a new town during a cold dark Midwestern January, I found myself enveloped in the light and warmth of his expanding being as he launched his journey into the greater beyond.

Differentiating Loss

Late-May

    Some people are aware right away of how they feel. Others are more mental or action-oriented, and must learn how to stop and listen to what is going on inside. I consider myself one of the latter, being both mental and action-oriented. In the Jungian sense, I call "feeling" my "inferior function": it operates strongly, but unconsciously, and therefore tends to dominate from below, creating a reactive and defensive attitude. I pray that, as I surrender to feelings and discover how to consciously navigate and integrate them, I will be gifted with a key that opens a door to becoming a whole human being.

    This experience of losing Jeff has plunged me headlong into the feeling world. So much of what goes on within me now is not rational or subject to my control. And of course, what "I" want more than anything is to control it, whatever it is, or at least to direct its course, to know I'm okay.

    But this feels like my old self talking. My new self, the one who has just been born, is yet relaxing in the feeling of being upheld and bathed in a supportive fluid from the very day Jeff died. And this subtle but steady feeling of unconditional support, I discover, carries with it a sense of okayness that my need for control has never satisfied. Indeed, this invisible lubrication felt essential when I had to keep myself together during three sudden shocking descents whose stories I will tell in this chapter.

I consider these three descents after his death to be the structural backbone of the body of my loss, which includes smaller descents as well as periods of great clarity and perspective. Time feels more elastic than usual, so that I experience the off/on alteration of up and down at varying speeds. My moods can gyrate wildly and precipitously or they can resemble the long slow swells and troughs of a heaving sea. In any case, the surface of this sea is subject to continuous perturbations.

What I am attempting to do is to be and to remain conscious, mindful, aware of my moods, especially of the darker moods as they build up inside. Loneliness, longing, numbness, futility—I want to catch their first subtle whisperings, so that I may learn to honor, deepen, and release them.

A dark mood usually tiptoes in with such stealth that only after some time am I aware of its presence. It is then that I notice I have been in a strange state for days, and am relieved to finally identify what has been gathering. "Aha! I am sad." Or, "Ah, yes, here it is again, melancholy." Or, maybe, "Here's that old feeling of abandonment come back to haunt me." Or, perhaps, "Wow . . . my body is experiencing desolation, awful, really icky, yucky—like coming off a psychoactive drug." Or, "Something weird is going on, I am feeling . . . what? *What?*"

I strive to catch the feeling, to name it. For, when I do notice and name it, then if I can go further and actually describe both the feeling and the exact situation in which it arises—the triggers are like spikes, pricking latent memories of scenes from our life together—the emotion moves. I notice that the emotion moves when I enter both feeling and memory fully, no matter how painful. I allow them in, I honor them. When fully acknowledged, I notice that the feeling subtly lifts, lightens, imperceptibly dissolves; this release diffuses into my whole self, moving *me* into a new space, a new reality.

In this way, maybe because I am deliberately sensitizing myself to be highly aware of the different faces of my grief, life does go on. So far, I seem to be bypassing the debilitating depression that I fear sometimes accompanies loss of a loved one.

I have only a few memories of our life in Indiana, since Jeff and I were together here such a short time before he died. (Remember, I came to Bloomington in late August to set up our household for the next three weeks, and then left for an extended visit with my children in Massachusetts. I returned after his heart attack, two days prior to death.) But there are a few Bloomington memories, which do easily trigger grief. When I return to the scenes of these memories, they help me to honor and discharge dark moods. Memories like walking through the Indiana University campus, especially in the evening. On my nighttime walks now, I recall our romantic dinners out, holding hands while strolling to and from our little house, savoring the beauty of the groomed, hardwood-tree-filled grounds of this spacious midwestern university.

I miss him then. My soul calls out to his then. I miss him. I just miss him. And I miss the protection of his bulky presence. Now I am a "woman alone," and notice that my hyper-alertness at night has returned, unbidden and unwelcome, to the level habitual pre-Jeff.

Sunday nature walks, ending with lunch out somewhere, activate another trigger. I continue this tradition that Jeff and I enjoyed most Sundays during our twelve years together; and though I could invite one of the few people I have met here to go with me, I need to experience these solo walks, and these solo lunches out, first. I need to remember who I am in the world as an individual, and these particular activities, which both remind me of him and offer contrast—because he is *not* walking, *not* eating out with me—both honor memory and push me into my own living presence.

We had stopped sleeping in the same bed years ago, so I don't need to get used to the absence of his body next to mine. We changed bed arrangements due, I said at the time, to his snoring, but also, I later admitted, to the fact that during menopause I found I needed to sleep in my own aura, with no "contamination" from another's presence. (His response was ambivalent: on the one hand, my need to sleep alone hurt him and he felt abandoned and unlovable—I could see it on his face, though he would never admit it; on the other hand, I could sense the underlying glee in this solitary man's nightly relief from daily togetherness. Of course he wouldn't admit that either.)

So different, my needs now! Had I undergone a husband's death in my twenties or thirties or forties I would have been much more devastated, as my being, during those decades, was in a state of chronic bending towards others. (And I would have never considered having my own bedroom.) My lifestyle, back then, was more interactive, and my condition that of a woman who needed the mirror of another to sense the reality of her own life.

Menopause changed all that. (And poor Jeff came to me as I was just beginning to encounter the storms of "the change.") Though still interactive, I now seek solitude. Though still needing stimulation, I now savor contemplation.

Jeff had greeted this gradual rebalancing of my fundamental needs with relief; he always enjoyed his own company, and unless interrupted, tended to move through his days in an extended state of meditation.

So we were becoming more alike in that way, and our marriage segued into the poet Rilke's description of a "good marriage" as one in which each "protects the other's solitude." I had long admired, but never, before marriage to Jeff, fully appreciated an expanded awareness that includes the Other but finds the origins of movement in one's own center.

And it's odd, but now that he is gone I seem to be even taking up some of his habits! I go to bed an hour or two later than before, echoing his greater aliveness during the dark hours. I said earlier, in a more mystical mood, that I sense his soul in mine and mine in his. Well, even on the level of daily life, I sense him in me. I now listen to opera, a source of contention between us. As soon as I left he would crank up Wagner or Mahler, and on my return I would interrupt his reverie, ask him to turn it down.

One time I told him that he used music as a substitute for human passion. I said it with a wistfulness that reflected all that had not transacted between us on the level of biological lovemaking. For he was not really interested in the sexual realm of companionship and that was hard on me, especially in the beginning, when I was in menopause, and highly sexed.

But he was decidedly sensual, and my physical/ emotional being came to savor this aspect of our relationship, and to value it as a worthy substitute; post-menopause, I convinced myself that it was actually preferable to the hormonal storms of lovemaking.

(Even after twelve years, the sight of Jeff coming up the walk, or into the room after some time apart, would make my heart flutter. The physical frisson between us was forever present, and palpable. I realize that my body still longs for his body; I acknowledge that even now it refuses to be consoled.)

After four months, I now know the triggers to plug into if I need to release a feeling building up inside. There are the evening walks through campus, the Sunday afternoons; there are other little triggers, like opening a closet that still contains his personal stuff to re-read one of his old childhood essays, or looking up at his beaming face I framed and placed above all the family photos on the wall, so that he shines down on us always. Plus, there are the little situations that catch me unaware, and when I look back on them I notice they are all first-time-post-mortem events. Like the other day when I was going through some packing material, and suddenly realized that he was the last person to touch this material. My breath caught in my hands, as I touched what he had last touched; an image of him patiently pawing through the styrofoam peanuts floated through, triggered a sudden momentary sob.

The more I retrace the steps we walked together, the more overlays of my own solo experience accrue to them, and grief gets tramped into mulch for new life.

I can usually decide when to release a dark mood. In fact, I can count on one hand those times when sudden strong moods have stolen up to knock me flat from behind—and these were all within the first two months. (I am not proud of this reserve; I only note it as an aspect of my German heritage.) For example, the afternoon several days after he died when my dear friend Claudia tried on his green pile jacket. She came through the door unexpectedly and what I saw was the jacket moving towards me, not her in it. There he was! I could feel Jeff in that jacket!

It was the surprising thrill of seeing/feeling him and, the very next second, the crashing disappointment that it wasn't him—it was that sudden, near-simultaneous ecstasy/

despair that threw me into a tailspin.

I prefer to do my weeping alone. That time I was caught off guard.

One might conclude that sorrow and happiness are alternate states that I plug into, almost at will. Yet it's not a matter of will, but of my willingness to follow feelings wherever they lead, and to slow down or speed up their expression, as I deem appropriate, depending on context. For me, happiness and sorrow in grief are best described as flips of a coin, and, predictably, at least so far, one always succeeds the other! Indeed, the physical expression of sorrow invariably ushers in a state of bliss, centering me within a fluidic atmosphere shining through the world.

That physical expression itself has changed from the first month when my sorrow would explode to primordial howling. Eventually it would calm into tears, but while it was going on I was astonished by the wild thrusts of extreme emotional purging, as forceful as diarrhea, or vomiting. This howling, or keening, was something I had never encountered in others, though I may have witnessed its power to galvanize a grieving widow in some obscure foreign film. This kind of eruption was not entirely foreign to me, however, for I remember standing by in awe, thirty years ago, as my body and vocal chords blew out immediately after hearing of my sister's cancer diagnosis.

This howling—how do I describe it? Like entering the zone of a Category Five hurricane which stretches the mouth into a giant "O" and zaps the body into total realignment; it's so strong and so uncontrollable that it feels like giving birth, where the body obeys its own laws and the conscious self is but an onlooker. That my body could periodically be so uncommonly expressive interested me, and I intuitively knew that it was helping me process my unfathomable loss by enlivening every cell to carry the memory.

As the weeks went on, the initial spasms softened into undulations, as repeated bursts invisibly carved containers holding sorrow into channels for sorrow's flow. I was grateful when I noticed tears starting to release more easily, and eventually, to pour down like rain.

This grief since Jeff's death has an entirely different feel from other occasions when I have "lost the man in my life." Not only does mourning the loss of Jeffrey seem to be essentially alien to those other griefs, but I can, I think—though maybe I speak too quickly—declare that this loss, though decidedly raw, does not usually render me exhausted and numb; nor does it echo the endless pain and suffering of those other losses. Finally, I notice that, unlike the loss of some former lovers, I have not—or not yet—entered the twilit dead zone, not been catapulted into the dark night of the soul.

This dissimilarity, on the face of it, surprises, since, unlike the others, I lost Jeffrey though actual physical death. He no longer walks this earth. I would think that my pain and suffering now would be infinitely greater than those others, but it is not—despite the fact that Jeff and I were together much longer than my other relationships, none of which lasted more than six years and most decidedly shorter.

Claudia thinks this differential is due to the fact that Jeff and I "actually accomplished something" in our relationship. That, unlike other relationships, we did not fail to connect; instead, we actually dared to suffer the humbling journey of cultivating the nectar of intimacy below the storms of egoic pride.

And it's true, while some areas of life remained unexplored, I feel immensely grateful that through our relationship Jeff and I did transform our individual selves into companions whose hearts gradually softened and opened to include each other and the world around.

My grief over the loss of Jeffrey not only differs from the loss of other primary males in my life, but differs as well from my experience of the deaths of a number of people who figured prominently in my life, all within the past few years. Their deaths all preceded Jeff's, but none of them prepared me for it. There seems to be no way to prepare for an individual death. Death is an encounter with the Real, and its hunger seems to be, at least in my experience, omnivorous.

Others who have died include Rhoda, Jeff's mother and my mother-in-law; Kathy, a sister-in-law; Shauna, a mentor; Ella, a long-term friend; and Patrick, my first husband and father of my children. Just as no two families or marriages or friendships are alike, so, for me, the death of each person held its own distinct flavor.

Rhoda carried the emotional lineage for her son. Like him, she too had bottled up her passion. Rhoda lived a life of quiet desperation until the final two years when she simply took to her bed more and more, and eventually refused to get up. "Senile depression," they called it. I call it a life-long grief that she could not move.

I always sensed that her death would be the key to unlock Jeff's passion, for she had psychically held him in her arms from the time he was born, and their relationship was one of unconscious emotional incest. No blame. As Rhoda and Jeff were one in their large-heartedness, so did they both find life in this competitive, cutthroat culture excruciating. The tie that held him to her was also the rose that bloomed, in secret, inside them both.

He was the glorious sun that rose and set in all of her days after seven married years of longing for children. The presence of little Jeffrey, who on emotional and physical planes was truly her inheritor, assuaged her chronic disappointment in the conditions of her life. And though she didn't realize it—she was a generous woman who welcomed me into her family's life with open arms— she also, as long as she was alive, would not, could not, let him go. He was his mother's boy.

Her death did trigger a greater aliveness, a further softening of his already large heart. It was as if his life was starting over, as he made plans to return to school. Then, slightly over two years later, it seems his life was complete! As Tasha, a very empathic friend, said: "He was rather like a flower, blooming ever so briefly with exquisite blossoming, and most of the time growing in hiding where only those who had eyes to see, might."

Kathy's and Ella's and Shauna's faces still swim into view on certain occasions—when I would like to share insights with the intense and intrepid Kathy; when I recall Ella's breezy optimism and our many hikes and horseback rides in the Idaho mountains; when I would like to discuss the past or the future of the Crone movement, which Shauna and I helped to spearhead together and in which she was for me a template for one who serves the cause of women. As one or more of their faces zooms in, I move into a melancholic mood that, however, passes swiftly.

When I think of Patrick, what comes up is much more complicated. Our marriage ended badly, after six years of incessant bickering, and towards the end, bitter and nasty fights with two small, disturbed children underfoot—one with facial tics and running wild, the other pale and withdrawn. I have been processing the tragedy of that broken early marriage and its effects on our sons for over thirty years, and the feeling tones infusing memories of Patrick have gone through several transmutations.

For the first fifteen years after our divorce I held him at arms' length, frozen in hatred and denial. Now I realize that my unconscious was protecting me; any link with him would have shut down the delicate process of initiating my own inner development.

The animosity between Patrick and myself did not even begin to move until my late thirties, when after decades of struggle and pain and victimization, I realized that my life was not working. I could sleepwalk no longer. Go any further in that direction, and I would fall off a cliff. Thus it was that sheer survival brought me face-to-face with the necessity of committing to the hard, long inner work of taking responsibility for all the choices in my life and tracing them to their roots in childhood and in my own nature.

In this work I discovered that Patrick was a placeholder for my father, his perfectionism and controlling nature an exact mirror for the early conditions to which I had been subservient externally while seething inside. Then I made the deeper discovery, the one that brought me to rock bottom: my father was a placeholder for the perfectionist, controlling aspects of my own nature, as projected, in denied form. Again, no blame. We were all doing what we were born to do in the best way we knew how at the time.

Gradually—and I mean over a period of many years after we separated—my feelings towards Patrick mutated. I began to acknowledge him as an important mentor. The example of his life taught me many things, including how to follow my own unique nature despite society's pressures to conform. And, more immediately, during the boiling cauldron that was our six-year marriage, his withering critiques forced me to learn how to stand up to him rather than be crushed. By the end, despite his volcanic fury and my own quivering knees, I had gained the nerve to choose a course other than the one he demanded.

Then followed twenty years of mutual hatred and recrimination.

The formal healing for this deeply stuck old karma came in a five-hour meeting with Patrick in 1987 to which my courageous mother agreed to come as witness. How that meeting came about, and what went on there, is wondrous and strange, best told at another time. I note here only that as I hugged him at the end of it his mouth was still cursing me yet his body was no longer frozen but vibrating, clinging.

Another decade went by with little contact between us, until the night, eighteen months ago, when I dreamed of Patrick's naked body lying on the floor in the dark. In the morning I told Jeff about the dream, and remarked, with wonder, "the body was empty." Instantly, Jeff responded: "You'd better get hold of your kids." I looked at him askance—"Really?"— not wanting to take the dream seriously. A few days later, without consciously remembering the dream, I tried to reach my older son in Massachusetts several times and his answering machine did not click on.

Then, about a week after the dream, I received my younger son's call announcing his father's death from a heart attack in the middle of the night. The coroner judged that death had occurred three days earlier. A Harvard student whom he had been mentoring found him naked on the floor, apparently on his way to the bathroom.

I notice that, when I mentioned the losses of women in my life I was able to instantly summarize something about each one and how she affected me. Then, when I began to talk about Patrick my tone changed; it quickly moved into the story of the mutational process in me triggered by our failure to connect. There seems to be a great difference between my relations with close women friends and those with male lovers. I would like to think that means my relations with women are not so karmically fraught, but I may be wrong. My own mother is still alive; I do not know what my response to her death will be. Perhaps my mourning for her will trigger a deeper mourning of the other female deaths than I have been able to access so far.

Speaking of recent deaths, there is one more that I hesitate to speak of, since some would call me irreverent or cruel or cold when I say that of all the deaths that preceded Jeffrey's, the most difficult for me was that of my cat, Lukas.

When I read it over, that sentence sounds silly even to me! But it's true. Each human's death brought shock, usually followed by a brief and mild ecstasy, when I seemed to sense his or her joy on the other side; then a melancholy would steal in periodically, but briefly, for a more or less protracted time. In contrast, the death of Lukas dropped me into a pit of desolation which I had trouble dispelling.

I talked with a friend, another animal lover, about this, and she said she responded in the same way when one of her horses died. And that, for her, the death of animals has been much more difficult than the death of people.

Lukas was my first cat. I only had him for eighteen months. He was an indoor/outdoor cat, and lived with Jeff and me in a yurt in the Wyoming mountains, surrounded by wild animals. Though I knew from the outset that there was a good chance Lukas would die at a young age—and I would say, breezily, that this might be the price I would pay for allowing him to live free—I was stunned to discover just how deeply we had bonded.

Lukas was a hunter who would disappear for

several days at a time; and he was a temple cat, a lap kitty, whose long direct gaze into my eyes unnerved me, blasted my awareness wide open.

Then came the beautiful spring morning when he pranced up to me in a manner very unlike him; he hopped and jumped and danced around my feet as if to shout a greeting that I would never forget. Little did I know that this was to be our last interaction.

Several days later, I was on a weekend journey far from home. I had called Jeff to hear that Lukas had disappeared. I went into such anxiety concerning his whereabouts and safety that I decided to go into meditation and ask his spirit to contact mine, to let me know if he was okay.

I did this in bed, before napping. At first I felt foolish, thinking it a futile project, that Lukas would not contact me, that I had no capacity to hook up in this way. But then, I reminded myself, Lukas would usually appear just when I was beginning to wonder where he was and before I called his name. In fact, I had often played a little game to see if he really was responding telepathically to my internal direction. Usually he did. I like to think that he sometimes didn't come because he was too far away, or because he was so involved in stalking some mouse or bird that he couldn't be bothered.

So now I was asking to get in touch, and specifically that Lukas give me information I could obtain in no other way. Was he alive? And if not, how did he die?

With these questions I settled back to meditate, but soon began to drift off. I was almost asleep when a hazy image swam into view. It was of a hillside meadow, with aspen groves marching up both sides. (I knew exactly where this hillside was, about two miles from the yurt.) As I became aware of being in reverie, I noticed that my point of view was close to the ground, and that I was moving uphill, when a dark shadow appeared on the ground in front of me and hovered just over my head and neck. Then, nothing.

I came out of this vision knowing that Lukas was dead, and deduced that a big bird had taken him. Most likely eagle or large hawk, since it was daytime in the vision, and owls are nocturnal.

Oddly enough, I discovered on arriving home that Jeff had also encountered the same strange vision while driving in his car.

Perhaps I felt the loss of Lukas so strongly because my bond with him was physical and emotional, not mental. Lukas had burrowed under my skin. Our connection felt deeper than language. Likewise my connection with Jeff. He was a man who seldom spoke, who held vast space inside him crowded with ideas and feelings, but rarely showed himself to others. I have always wondered whether the high blood pressure such people sometimes develop has to do with this feeling of bursting with something that can't quite be born.

This brings me finally to the three cataclysmic descents that I mentioned at the beginning of this chapter. They are the primary motivation for my need to clearly differentiate loss, and especially to ask the question: what is mine, what is not? For I believe that during these past four months there have been times when Jeff's spirit has actually utilized my body to help clear emotions which, in this earthly life, had been stuck inside him.

Jeff was in an expanded state prior to death; many people told stories of seeing or feeling or vicariously experiencing his flight from earth in a state of bliss and joy, free as a bird. I too was caught up in that ecstatic state, for weeks. However, I must also report that, given my experience of these three descents, I also believe that Jeff then had to double back in order to finish his own work. But of course I don't really know this. All I know is that in order to begin to comprehend what happened to me I need to perceive it, and what I see as his part in it, in a certain manner. No doubt the reality is way bigger than anything I can imagine.

Thus, I perceive that though he may have been done spiritually, he was not done emotionally; that he had to immerse himself one final time, even after he "died," in this dense realm of Earth and its Moon which governs both the swings of the tides and our capacity to cycle through emotion.

Each of the three occasions that created what I call this structural backbone to the body of my loss (and his?) occurred during a time when I was wrapping up a specific aspect of his life to which he was deeply attached. These three occasions were all prompted during the two months I was wrestling with his enormous collections.

The first occasion took place the evening I worked with the final box of music CDs. I had spent many hours on this project of carefully packing thirty boxes for shipment to a New York music store. Now when I recall that evening, I am struck by the realization that this was the first time I was listening to music. Those first post-Jeff months had been observed in silence. I had turned on the radio to NPR just as it announced a composition by Elgar, a cello concerto. I had not remembered hearing and appreciating Elgar before this evening, and it seemed as if I was listening with Jeffrey's ears, immersed in the big, sonorous, lyrical lines, how they seemed to carry tragic human emotions from centuries upon centuries of conflict. As incomprehensibly large were the passions invoked, so Jeffrey's precise and discerning intelligence was also present, following the various melodies and tonalities in their separate yet unified threads, all at once.

As "Jeff," I seemed to be both absorbing much more information than usual, and accessing much more emotion than my own small body was capable of sustaining.

As I began to pack this final box the tears began, so copious that afterwards I felt as if my body had been drained of fluid. The music opened me to cry without howling first as prelude, and the release felt both delicious and terribly sad. Images floated through—of Jeff trying to bring his voice back with a coach these last few years and failing; of Jeff listening, always listening to music while on the computer, usually through headphones if I was around; of Jeff's giant gong, his clarinet, his trumpet, his harp, his keyboard, drums of all kinds; of Jeff's youthful dreams of becoming a composer or, at the very least, a conductor; of the yellowing original compositions saved from his high school years that I had found buried inside the book boxes. (These compositions were "difficult" according to his voice teacher, to whom I sent them: "eight-part choral arrangements with huge three-octave spans. But isn't that just like him?" We both laughed to think of the adolescent Jeff showing off.)

By now I was in a swirling current, held in Elgar's slow, wide, noble river. The music and my mood were dovetailing exactly. Perhaps the music triggered the mood, or perhaps the music was the mood. In any case, my appreciation that evening of the music and the mood felt all-encompassing.

That was the first incident where I felt my body moving an emotional current larger than my own. I had sensed, early in my grieving process, that he and I would continue our connection; that though he was no longer incorporated, our work would go on. I realize that this thought might reflect the "grieving widow's" need to hold on. Either way, it does not matter. The experience feels so strong that I have no choice but to go with it until it is truly over.

These three descents have left me with the feeling that, if he and I do have common work, this work involved, initially, the use of my body as a carrier for powerful emotions he apparently needed to move through in the early stages post-death. And I feel that I, too, needed this interdimensional tranfusion to finally immerse myself in the whole of his being. My own being was not equipped to experience the power and intensity of his frequency while he was alive. I shudder to realize how lonely he must have felt. He had to leave this world for me to find him.

As usual, the timing feels uncanny. Three years ago I began, with his encouragement, to learn the arts of chi kung and tai chi. Now, looking back, I see that this teaching prepared me for this massive transfusion from Jeff's reality. Thanks to these daily physical practices my body has become strong and flexible enough to briefly carry such a current without bursting into flame.

And I treasure what remains, what has evolved in me since his death. This is very hard to describe (as are all these "feelings"). My attempt to integrate my new experience of Jeffrey seems to be re-organizing my inherent structure. For example, I tell my friends that in writing about these experiences, my circumference has expanded; I feel energy channeling through a fire hose rather than a garden hose.

The second descent occurred a week or so later. I was in the final stages of the basement book collection project, opening each box, handling each book to decide which ones I wanted to keep, arranging others in piles of various kinds—Music, Math and Science, Russian, Miscellaneous Literature A and B were the categories—and carefully repacking them in new, labeled boxes. I think I already mentioned that what had started out as a job done with great resentment toward this man who allowed himself to get so attached to so much and leave me with the remains transformed into a long, winding healing journey as I discovered the breadth and depth of the far-ranging and unusual worlds his giant brain and mind had absorbed.

I came across many three-ring binders as well, documenting contents of various trainings he had taken, mostly in alternative healing methodologies. These I would open to remove the paper for recycling. On one particular day I was taking apart a Trager instruction book, also in a binder, and besides paper, it was categorized with plastic pages, so took more differentiation than usual to recycle.

I sat down on the basement stairs, preparing to go through this binder slowly, page by page. Just setting that intention was enough to trigger a tsunami of grief. I felt my body being galvanized, forcefully expanding into a conduit larger than that for which it was originally designed. After I don't know how long, my body finally calmed down and I "woke up" to find myself rocking back and forth, eyes blurry and overflowing, taking page after page, separating plastic from paper. This time I was not surprised. I had already been "used" in this way once before. And germane to this occasion is the fact that Milton Trager, the founder of Trager bodywork, had been Jeff's beloved mentor. Besides attending countless Trager trainings, Jeff had tutored others in the Trager method and worked part-time as a Trager practitioner for nearly two decades. I sensed that Milton was an anchor in his life, a model to follow, a good father.

A number of times over the years, Jeff had been

pleased to tell me how other students of Milton said that Jeff reminded them of him. Indeed, the two did look alike, with bald heads ringed by grey/white curls and big frames trailing unusually long arms. Moreover, Jeff's huge energy and quiet ways were also, apparently, similar to those of Milton.

But there was one crucial difference between them, which I noted in the photos of Milton. I loved to look at these photos, since Milton's face was capable of just about any human expression, all of them suffused with compassion. In contrast, not until his final weeks did Jeff's face relax, broaden, and release into extended mobility, enabling him to continuously radiate inner peace, joy and love into the world. Indeed, in years past Jeff had bragged about his inscrutable poker face, obviously relishing the fact that no one could tell what he was thinking or feeling. So I had always been struck by both the obvious similarities as well as what was, to me, this glaring contrast between Jeff and his beloved mentor.

Thus I was not at all surprised to be engulfed by another huge emotional purge during the dismantling of that Trager manual. It felt as if I were dismembering Jeff's body, what had held him together all those years, the lineage he had been following, the intention he had unconsciously set and in the very end did gloriously succeed in creating within his own corporeal being.

I come now to the third and final occasion, what I look back on now as the finale of what I imagine as the first stage of my own—and perhaps the final stage of his—grieving process.

Several dealers were interested in parts of Jeff's collection. One would have purchased the thirty boxes of math books, another, the eighteen boxes of music books. But one used-and-rare book dealer showed an interest in the entire collection, and in fact declared that he would make the trip himself to come get it. Dean had called me from Jackson Hole a few days after Jeff died to tell me that he owed me $500, due to an uncompleted transaction between Jeff and himself when we left Jackson for Bloomington. He also said that, when the time came, he would love to purchase Jeff's entire collection, that he had been working with him for a few years, and every time Jeff brought books in he would want 95% of them. So, Dean said, he knew the quality and range of Jeff's mind as well as his discriminating taste in books.

We set a date, April 28, for him to fly out here, rent a large truck to transport the enormous weight of 210 boxes of books, and drive back to Jackson.

I very much looked forward to Dean's arrival, and anticipated my relief as I handed over this book collection which had felt like a great weight holding Jeff down when he was alive and an albatross around my neck since his death. I planned to spend three days with Dean, figuring it would take him that long to sample what was in the boxes and give me a price based on what he found.

Even the process of selling the books, in other words, would take a long time. Imagine my surprise, then, when Dean came upstairs after only a few hours and announced that he was done figuring, and that he would give me $15,000 for the entire collection! I was not surprised by the price, as others had estimated the math alone at $7,000, but I was extremely surprised by the speed. And that was only the first event of a day that sped by and seemed graced with magic. Everything fell into place: he could pick up the truck that same day instead of the next; college students in the neighborhood were glad to earn money moving the books from the basement to the truck so we "old people" wouldn't have to; we even had time for a walk through campus and a leisurely restaurant dinner.

All day long, concerned for my feelings, Dean kept asking, "Are you sure you're okay with this?" and I would insist, "*Yes!*" emphatically. But when the check had left his hands for mine and been ceremoniously put in the bank, I began to feel strange. It was hard to put my finger on what exactly was going on within me, but finally, when he asked the question again at dinner, I said, "Actually, I feel weird. I thought I would feel relieved, and I do. But a bigger part of me feels unmoored; what I thought was an albatross turns out to have been an anchor, something I needed."

That evening, after Dean had driven off to his motel in the loaded truck, I felt agitated. The agitation lasted all night long, in fact reminding me of the very first night after Jeff died: tossing and turning, insomniac, having to go to the bathroom more than usual, and above all, that staticky state of constant unrest.

By the next morning my nervous system was totally out of whack, and I hoped my usual early morning routine of yoga, chi kung, and tai chi would bring me back into balance.

I did my practices, and they didn't help. I was still in a terrible state.

Next I sat down at the computer to work on an essay. No good. Couldn't concentrate.

Finally, at 10:00 A.M., I decided that I might as well just take a nap, despite the odd hour. I didn't sleep during my "nap," but apparently my mind did empty enough so that by the time I arose, an hour later, a new thought floated through—one that I knew, intuitively, I had to act on immediately.

"I need to do ceremony," I announced to myself, "to clear the emotional residue from the basement."

Once my mind was informed, it was as if my body knew exactly what to do. First I would burn the pages from the spiral notebook in which I had documented the boxes in their categories; then I would smudge the basement with burning sage to cleanse it.

I tore out the five pages from the notebook and took matches outside. Casting about for privacy from neighbors, I finally decided on the covered stairs to the basement. I sat down and lit the first page, which took a long time to curl and blacken. The humidity slowed things down, and the slow process slowed me down. By the time the final page had turned to ash I had settled into an altered state appropriate for ceremony.

Next I took sage and other smudging herbs down into the basement. As I walked down the stairs I looked over to the large area where the book boxes had been stacked, four or five deep, and noticed that there was indeed a nearly visible heavy miasmic emotional cloud suspended in the air, so thick it was almost palpable.

I lit the herbs and began by walking around the entire basement, then finally closed in on the area where the boxes had been stacked. As I circled this area I began to chant, "Let go, let go, let go! Let go! *Let go*!" over and over again. The chants quickly transformed into sobs, then howls, as my body spiraled into a whirling dervish, whipping around "out of control" and violently flinging off waves of feeling. Had anyone come upon me, they would have thought me mad. And I *was* a mad woman, the only difference being that a tiny potent light of awareness within me witnessed the entire drama.

(Now I realize, at least in part, why I have been so very adamant that I do my grieving in solitude. Grief, of course, is a natural process, and it seems to take different forms depending on the nature of the person in whom great loss is being processed and integrated. Yet, in our culture, we tend to tell those in mourning to make sure they surround themselves with family and friends. But if somebody else is present, grief doesn't proceed in its own unique manner, because we affect one another. Ancient cultures seem to respect death more, and its effects upon the living. They recognize that a person in grief inhabits a different world, set apart from others. In the villages of Greece, for example, even now widows dress in black and sequester themselves for a certain period of time. One can argue that they sometimes go to the other extreme, dressing in black for decades. In any case, in this country, just as we are terrified of aging, dying, and death, so our grief is often stopped or stopped up or managed, somehow, pharmaceutically or otherwise. We end up like Jeff's mother, depressed. I am determined not to let that happen.)

This phase of the final purgation of Jeff's attachment to the experimental ideas and mathematical, musical, scientific, religious and historical facts and theories and, of course, literary beauty—all in many languages— that he had gathered and nourished internally during fifty-five years of life took about half an hour. (Oops! "That's all?!" I hear him ask, amazed and upset by how quickly I dispatched with his great mass of emotional residue, thinking my haste irreverent, downright sacrilegious.) By the end the space felt cleared and I utterly depleted and exhausted.

I slept well that night, and the next day I felt as if reborn.

Several days later Dean called to say he and the loaded truck had arrived safely in Jackson. Then he told me a story, one that holds special interest for me because Dean is decidedly not a person who traffics in unseen energies. Indeed, during our one day together he had looked at me blankly when I started to tell of mysterious "phenomena" that had accompanied Jeff's death, and so I quickly stopped.

"I arrived home around noon," Dean began. "My son and his friends unloaded the truck and hauled the boxes upstairs into the storage room over the bookstore. Then we went out to dinner. When I came back I started to open the music boxes. All went really well until I came to the final box, when I started to get a really weird feeling. The feeling was so strong that I found myself saying, out loud, 'It's okay, Jeff, they are all going to good homes.'"

Addendum, June 16: It has now been over five months since Jeff died. I just spent twelve days in Jackson, where we held a beautiful heartfelt memorial for him and, among other visits, I stopped into Dean's bookstore. He took me upstairs to the storeroom to show me what remained to be unpacked, proudly pointing to a paltry pile of about twenty boxes. Then he indicated a spot on the floor by a desk, where eight to ten mailers were piled, ready to go out. All were Jeff's books, he said, sold that morning over the Internet. He picked them up and read off their labels, one by one: "India, South Korea, Japan, Germany, Brazil, South Africa. . . ."

Much as, a week after he died, I had a vision of Jeff's spirit holding the Earth in his belly, so now his beloved books circle the world.

The Memorial

Early-June

On May 31, I stood in line at Indianapolis International Airport for the flight to Jackson Hole and Jeff's memorial. The ashes were with me. Given new security procedures, I had decided to accompany the ashes rather than bury them in to-be-inspected checked baggage.

I stood in the security line for thirty minutes, grateful for the wheeled carry-on. (It's surprising what cremains weigh! One would think a pile of dust from even big-boned Jeff would be pillow-light.)

Finally the line branched into six security stations. I heaved Birkenstocks, small backpack and wheeled case on the rolling conveyor belt and walked through.

"What is *that*?!" the female guard asked loudly, incredulous, as she pushed the button to stop the belt. "It's my husband!" I announced, relishing her shock. (When I tell this story to others, that is what I say—for its comic effect. But what I actually said in that moment was, "It's my husband's cremains," in a tremulous voice.)

A male guard boomed, in an official tone, "Do you have a letter?" "A letter?!" I asked, stumped. "Yes, from the crematory." "Noooo," I stammered, "but the ashes are in a tin, sealed in a box clearly labeled by the crematory." I'm sure my face conveyed anxiety. But, as usual, the new-widow's-halo smoothed the way. "Okay. You're okay," he said, in a kinder tone, as he pushed the button to restart the belt.

Just then the female guard blurted, "Is *that* the same *guy*?!"—of course a complete surprise to me and other travelers and guards whose ears had been leaning into this exchange. The male guard, glancing at the confusion on my face, said to her, "No, a different guy." And then, to me, "You are the second widow whose husband's cremains went through this station this morning, after not one in this entire airport for months!"

Jeff's death did what many deaths do; it brought people together who otherwise would not have met. Not only at the security station and during other unusual groupings, but of course at the memorial, and at a family dinner the night before, where his twin sisters met a few members of my extensive clan for the first time.

The memorial itself struck just the right tone; we were enveloped in an expansive loving energy that a number of people identified as Jeff's aura. My niece Megan saw him on the roof with a glorious angel, laughing and joking. Another woman saw him standing by me during the service, and then he was with her, his hands on her head. She told me later the people sitting next to her probably wondered why she suddenly started bawling. She also said Jeff let her know that he had taken the opportunity to leave this life when it presented itself; that it was fine, he was done; there was nothing more for him to do here.

We had decided to group the chairs in concentric circles, with a sweet altar in the middle created from moss and pansies, holding the gold can with his ashes and embellished with photos of him and a few of his large crystals and animal figurines and, of course, the beloved candy bars which contributed to his weight and, perhaps, his death. (I brought home the gold can to keep sweets in for visitors who wish to indulge in remembrance. When

I mentioned this to Jeff's dad, his sad face brightened: "That's what Rhoda used to do, keep sweets in a special jar for visitors!")

At the door, as people entered, stood a guest-signing table with memorabilia. Jeff's right-brain calling cards, "Circumconscious Navigations." (I couldn't find his left-brain cards). A few of his "A++!" essays and science projects from high school. Most noticeable: a massive and beautiful handmade paper, handstitched volume, which had started out to be a scrapbook and evolved into what I named, in awe, "The Book of Jeff."

My artistic niece Megan had assembled this treasury from photos, letters, poems, notes, other bits and pieces of his life that I had found buried here and there inside the basement book boxes. She said that the project, which took an entire month, "put itself together;" that working on the Jeff Book allowed her to enter his complex inner life and transformed her former fear of him as "intimidating."

The service, held in a Presbyterian church, was eclectic, in keeping with Jeff's omnivorous perspective. He had helped to establish the Jewish community of Jackson Hole, and the local rabbi was there to officiate. Jeff was a long-term member of the International Network for the Dances of Universal Peace (a world-wide organization with Sufi roots that honors all religions), so we would end with a circle dance to lyrics by St. Francis of Assisi.

We took a risk in asking the group of perhaps 100 people to stand up to sing and dance at the finale of Jeff's ceremony, and were surprised when most people did join in. In fact, a number of them told the dance leaders afterwards that they wished the dance had gone on longer; they would have liked to encounter the soul in the eyes of every single person in their circle.

I think the group's willingness to drop the mask and dance in this intimate, vulnerable way, singing, "Lord make me an instrument, of thy peace . . ." is a tribute to the atmosphere engendered by our stories of Jeff, and by what his life and death inspired.

The testimonials to him were of course many and varied, and we laughed and cried in equal measure. I had decided not to speak at his ceremony, until one woman who had danced with him as the gussied-up 19th century grandfather in the local Christmas *Nutcracker Suite* got up. Susan remarked on how quick on his feet, how flexible and limber he had been. At this I jumped up to relate how, on a family cruise for my parents' fiftieth wedding anniversary, my sister Mary had come upon Jeff in the pool area, biting his toenails. My remark was met by shocked silence—then a burst of laughter at the image of a large, Buddha-bellied, middle-aged man bringing toes to mouth.

Jeff, with a big baby body, was as limber as a baby. At the Indiana University memorial in January, I had wanted to call attention to his essential innocence, and surprised myself by referring to him as a "big baby!" We all laughed, a bit startled to recognize this truth. And many times over the years he had seemed to me like a five-year-old boy. So curious and vulnerable! So sweetly smiling. That innocence was an aspect of his nature not usually on display to the world, for which he had cultivated inscrutability—and if that didn't work, what I called "the baleful glare."

(One of our long-running sources of humor was of me trying to adopt "the glare." I would compose my mercurial face, tuck chin in, and try to both deaden my eyes while driving a fierce energy stream from them. It never worked. Even Mr. Inscrutable would crack up laughing.)

There were many tales, of course, of his seemingly limitless learning, of how there didn't seem to be any subject of which he didn't know more than anyone else. These stories were told with humor and fondness, in keeping with the patina of praise that blankets memorials—I chose not to bring up the times when others had felt intimidated and even annoyed. How often, I thought to myself, did I have to remind him, "Knowing a lot and being a know-it-all are two different things"?

His sister Andrea told a funny childhood story that illustrates what I imagine was one of the few times Jeff's mind was roundly defeated. He had gone into the kitchen for a snack and his mother was there. He asked her how much she knew about algebra, and she said "Nothing!" "Well then, trigonometry?" "Nothing!" On and on, he kept grilling her on various subjects, and the response was always "Nothing."

I winced to hear Andrea relate what he said next: "Well, then, if you don't know anything, what good are you?"

At this point I imagine his mother stopped rolling out pie dough as her big brown eyes bore into his, so like her own: "I know how to make a baby, and that is something you will never know!"

At the IU memorial students had spoken of his "humility." I was startled that they saw him this way, since he had five planets in Leo and a life-long tendency to either lord it over others or retreat into shyness. As an intellectual, Jeff felt especially uncomfortable in Jackson, a hard-bodied resort town. He and I were able to move below the encyclopedic part of him, but I know a number of Jackson people who found Jeff mentally overbearing. So when the rabbi, a truly humble man, also remarked on Jeff's humility in study group, where of course he knew more than the rabbi yet "offered his ideas quietly and in a spirit of genuine openness," again I was startled. Perhaps he could relax in a group of fellow Jews whose culture held a deep respect for learning.

Another burst of laughter greeted one of Jeff's fellow Jews, when he shared an email Jeff sent him shortly after applying to law schools. "I don't know where I'll get in," he wrote. "My undergraduate grades at Princeton were none too good, as I spent most of my time there in an altered state!"

(Even his excursions into altered states were prodigious. He told me that during college years he once spent two weeks high on LSD without sleep, each time taking another hit just as he was coming down from the previous one. "I used to have a better memory," he would conclude, "until I took all that acid." I would retort that maybe he had *needed* to slough off some of those brain cells.)

I do feel that any equanimity Jeff gained in sharing his knowledge with others was hard-won. He was a sensitive being, and he stuttered, especially in the presence of those who he sensed were judging him. Or, he would talk so fast and in such a mutter that no one could catch the meaning and didn't dare ask him to repeat.

So, more often than not, Jeff just didn't say anything. Why start? I bet he *did* know more than anyone else in Jackson Hole on any subject that interested him. ("But so what?" I would snap: "I bet your heart is even bigger than your brain.") I imagine his former communities—Ann Arbor, Cambridge, Paris, and Berlin— were more welcoming to this Renaissance man whose intelligence, to his deep disappointment, was barely utilized in our mountain community.

There were plenty of people in Jackson, however,

who could relate to him musically. The memorial itself started with the members of his Native American drum group drumming outside as people entered. Inside, Jeff's friend Gregory bathed them in a Bach cello concerto. Right after the rabbi's welcome we sang the Hebrew chant, from Psalm 133, "Heenay Matov": "Oh how wonderful it is for brothers and sisters to live together in peace!" Jeff's former choir members sang a local favorite, "God Be in My Heart." And my brother Mark with his guitar sang the old 'sixtys song, "Come Together Now."

For me, the most memorable music was offered by his voice coach, an eighty-year-old elder who came to Jackson from New York thirty years ago having already lived one professional lifetime in music. Prior to the service, his young wife told me that Jeff's death had made a great impact on Bob, that he had talked about Jeff every single day since he died. Bob spoke to us about how much he loved Jeff, and about how challenging he had been to teach because of the vastness of his musical learning and his great vocal range. In his youth, Bob told us, Jeff had learned to sing every aria from every opera: bass, baritone, tenor, alto, soprano—"even coloratura soprano!"

Invoking Jeff's help, his teacher then turned to signal the pianist accompanying him, and launched into a difficult aria from the opera *Manon* which, he said, was one of Jeff's favorites. It was a piece that, Bob told us, contained the entire range of what had been Jeff's voice when young, and the last piece he'd worked on before leaving Jackson. *They* sang that song, and though the "passage" notes from one vocal area to another were sometimes strained and imperfect, it didn't matter. The song was full, sensitive, exquisitely expressive—what Jeff had attempted, and with Bob as partner he now accomplished.

(The next day my friend Clarissa mentioned that Bob seemed very different now, bigger somehow, fuller. She said she felt Bob had incorporated some of Jeff's reality. When I related this story to my son Sean, he said that at one point during the meal following the memorial my granddaughter Kiera had cried, "I want Papa Jeff! I want Papa Jeff!" Sean told her Jeff wasn't there. "Yes, he is! There!" she cried, pointing to Bob.)

At the end of the service, immediately prior to the peace dance, a good friend of ours, one of three we had asked to witness our very private wedding ten years earlier, recited a poem in honor of Jeff which she had composed that week, less than a month after her own mother died. Lyn told me privately that she had asked Jeff to be with her during her mother's transition, and had felt his presence. "He was very helpful," she said, eyes welling with tears.

Jeff's twin sisters, Andrea and Stephanie, generously provided a catered dinner afterwards for all who attended.

Andrea remarked recently how much she appreciated those who came up to tell her of what she called "Jeff's accomplishments." Then, in a tone both empathic and distraught: "I had no idea how much he did for others. It would have been nice to know—he never let us in. Why didn't he share any of this with us? I thought I had a good relationship with my brother and felt like I was seeing him for the first time."

Andrea had arranged for each table to be graced with a beautiful basket of flowers. A little "flying Jeff" puppet peeked out from the flowers in each basket, to honor those who'd had visions of Jeff in a long gown, balding with grey/white curls streaming, ascending, free at last, full of joy. At the evening's end I distributed the baskets and puppets to some of Jeff's favorite people.

I had been quite tense in the days and nights

prior to the memorial, having trouble sleeping, needing to steal off for time alone, trying to center myself for the coming event. I didn't realize just how anxious I was until afterwards, when I poured myself a glass of wine and relaxed, staying up later than usual.

But even then my relaxation had an edge, again something I didn't realize until the next night, when the entire closing ceremony was truly over and I finally fell into soundless sleep.

Jeff's will specified that his ashes be given to the Snake and Gros Ventre rivers, both defining features of the Jackson Hole valley.

As a child Jeff had devoured the journals of Lewis and Clark; ever since then, he told me many times, he had wanted to live near the Snake River. Even his childhood home, in South Orange, New Jersey, had been located on "Wyoming Avenue"! So when I called him to me from Michigan in 1990, it felt like destiny.

The Snake had carved its channel at the foot of the Tetons, and the Gros Ventre mountains ran parallel to it, across the valley to the south. The yurts stood in the village of Kelly, directly on the Gros Ventre which emptied into the Snake a few miles down. Jeff and I had walked the Gros Ventre river trail hundreds of times, especially in spring, fascinated to observe runoff from mountain snowfields gradually carve new channels and islands over time.

Sometimes on our walks, to get him to talk to me, I would ask a question. Something, for example, about the mathematics of "turbulence in fluid flows" (I learned to call it that). He would stop, point to a line of bubbles and the intricacies of the surrounding currents, the location and geometry of nearby gravel bars; then he would happily expound, relieved to have been asked for a tiny morsel of what filled him inside.

It would take effort to ask him such a question, and I wasn't always up for it. Because of course he muttered, and I had to lean in and pay close attention to his gesticulations. Yet try as I might I could hardly understand him, though glimmers of wild startled meaning did sometimes flit by. I had a sense that, for Jeff, to wander in the higher reaches of mathematics was to enter worlds akin to exotic scenes in the fantasy novels he gave away, two each week, after reading them. There were times when I felt jealous of his near-continual reverie. I would say his name or touch him on the shoulder and invariably, he would look startled and at times annoyed to be called back. (How much of his love of mathematics was related to his need to be alone? How much of his aloneness was inevitable, given his love for mathematics?)

What little I could understand of his responses to my occasional questions was invariably interesting; I would come away with a frustrated, bittersweet feeling: if only I had more time or more patience or a better background, or a larger supply of sheer native intelligence. . . . I could learn so much from him.

That feeling has only increased since the day Jeff died. I miss having my own personal encyclopedia, my own living library and fact checker. Like everyone else, I had only scratched the surface of what he had to offer.

(It is interesting to note that in the weeks and months before he died, the muttering cleared up; his IU professors told me that he always raised his hand in class, and that what he had to say was expressive, well-informed and interesting; Claudia and others remarked on how, even on the telephone, they could now understand what he was saying!)

It is tempting to view Jeff as if he were one of the many people whose gifts are underutilized in life. His own father lamented to me that it was "too bad Jeff didn't find a way to make a contribution to society."

This remark holds unusual resonance coming from Amos Joel, a man who, while working for Bell Labs, invented the cell phone, holds over seventy other telecommunications patents, and received numerous national and international prizes. Everywhere Jeff's father goes he sees cell phones plugged to people's ears, and is constantly reminded of his contribution to society.

The sudden unexpected death of his son was, of course, a crippling blow for this eighty-five-year-old man who naturally took his son's weekly phone calls and twice-yearly visits for granted. I flew to New Jersey to visit Amos recently, and recognized that Jeff's death has precipitated a miraculous heart opening, releasing a grief that still seems endless: "I always feel," he told me, teary-eyed, "that I need another good cry."

Amos now worries that he was not a good enough father to Jeff, and worries that Jeff may have been "jealous" of his "success." A photo of Jeff comes to mind here: he is sitting on a chair in the Rose Garden of the White House, looking both acutely uncomfortable and resigned in his brand new suit, on the occasion when his father received the 1993 National Medal of Technology from President Clinton.

Given his father's cultural eminence, what could Jeff have done to equal him? Imagine how heavy were the family expectations for this first born, and only, son whom his parents and teachers all labeled a "genius;" "the smartest person," said one teacher, "to ever come through this high school."

Shall I label Jeff as yet another rising young star bent low by his status as son-of-the-great-man? Indeed, at times I do tend to fall into this cultural trap. But then I turn from this superficial perspective and sink into the vastness of Jeff's nature, essentially one of "being," not "doing;" and I rise to view our twelve years together as a trajectory whose velocity was at first slow and lugubrious, and by the end had amped up to warp speed. I sense that he had been caught, here below, in painful karmic traps from the deep, deep past; somehow our life together helped release him, so that by the time he left me, in shock shot through with ecstasy, I was stunned to notice his mastery of the art of letting go. Here was one more paradox: this man who had been so weighed down by matter could, with such perfection in timing, prove so free, so fast.

From artifacts I found after he died, I learned that he had long wanted partnership, and that, as an essentially passive person, he knew he needed someone who would draw him out. This confirmed my sense of him as, from the beginning of our time together, determined to follow our relationship through. His determination was my security. I could trust that I had at last attracted a partner who would be there, no matter what I threw at him, no matter how difficult and protracted our ego struggle. He was a man who would shift in resonance with my shifts, who would respond rather than refuse, when, periodically, I found myself internally prompted to explore yet another unknown dimension of my own unfolding nature.

I remember one time when I felt something building up inside me, and whatever it was, it made me feel cold and bored. Finally I noticed the feeling, and knew it meant I was about to undergo a shift of some kind. I told him so, and whispered, plaintively: "I hope you're coming with me." That was on a Saturday night. On Monday he started swimming, a practice he continued for many years, four or five times weekly, until we left Wyoming. Swimming increased his vitality, and was perhaps the most dramatic of his shifts in response to mine—but far from the only one.

Though his ego worried about and defended against being controlled (and my ego worried about and defended against his critiques) we both worked hard (with, of course, limited success) to transform aspects of our personalities that the other found impossible to live with. And though our rhythms were diametrically opposed, with me lightening fast and him at moving at a glacial pace— "like turning the Queen Mary," I would say, sometimes with affection and more often irritated—I was never in doubt of his abiding desire, through relationship with me, to gradually bring the various and paradoxical aspects of his largely submerged being into conscious awareness and attempt to integrate them.

It was, I feel, that work of bringing what had been held in darkness into the light of compassion for *himself*, and not just for others, which ultimately broke his karmic chains and allowed him to leave. (Had I known death would result from his work on himself, would I have resisted the work? Most likely. I sense that our souls' contract was for me to remain ignorant so that he could leave unimpeded. Aren't we all in that place with those we love?)

Our intense and continuous interpersonal work gradually improved our social life: over the years, and little by little, he left his isolated perch to develop a genuine interest in the small daily joys and sorrows of those with whom we began to share meals, or ski, or hike, or travel. The man came to me a brain; he left a human being.

And I am still astonished to recall the extraordinary expansion of the final few weeks and months of his life. Intuitively, I rest in the assurance that Jeff's greatest gifts were of the heart and spirit, that his overwhelming intellect was both boon and burden to his soul's path. Throughout his lifetime he was weighed down by cultural expectations that his (mental) genius bear (cultural) fruit, and yet, once he died, many of those who knew and loved him opened to new understanding of him.

Yes, it took his death for many of us to put his life in context. He was so quiet, so content, for the most part, to be left alone, and yet his large silent presence had such a decided effect on so many communities. One of my brothers remarked to me that while Jeff was too shy and quiet to feel at ease in our large boisterous family, what he did do was to serve as a guardian, watching over us all. And, as one woman quietly remarked at his memorial: "Jeff was a person who could sit in silence and in doing so open up enormous space."

When I mentioned her remark to Jeff's dad, his face lit up: "Ah, like John Cage. That's what he did. Opened up space through silence." (Amos had been introduced to John Cage the year they shared the Kyoto Prize, in Japan.)

I find it interesting that his father immediately compared Jeff to Cage, and am sad to realize once again how little his father understood him, and how hard that must have been for Jeff, who cared so much and wanted so much to have a real connection to his father. For when I think of how Cage created space and how Jeff created space—so different! John Cage created space between sounds; Jeffrey Joel created space in the atmosphere in which sounds are held.

Amos needs the reassurance of cultural acknowledgement of his worth, and he would have liked that for his son. Jeff's ego also needed acknowledgement, of course, but not so much as his father assumes; Jeff's home range was the inner life, and he dwelled mostly there, in the mystery.

Not until Jeff was no longer present in the flesh

did we realize the greatness of this man whose energies operated below culture, below even his enormous learning: his genius served the invisible planes. It was only in the finale of his life that his entire trajectory revealed shape and focus, allowing us to see that all along he had been doing what he needed to do in order to fulfill his particular destiny. Indeed, Jeffrey's life reminds us of the greater life that lives within and below cultural artifacts of any kind. His was the comfort of the Void; his was the Abiding Presence; his was the Buddhist Compassion; and I sense that I, along with many others, will continue to draw on Jeff's energy to help me move into that spaciousness he so naturally inhabited.

Thus, though Jeff did not "make a contribution to society" that can be measured in the usual ways, his situation differed profoundly from people who seem to live on the surface of their beings, creatures of culture and conditioning with no clue to the invisible seeds of treasure that await germination. Unlike those who never find the key to their interior lives, Jeff's inner gifts were fully developed; his struggle was with his difficult personality. He attempted, and if his expanded presence at the end of his life is any indication, in the end succeeded in surrendering his personal will to divine intention. During those few weeks and months leading to his death, his openhearted radiance warmed everyone fortunate enough to cross his path.

The Ashes

Mid-June

As in the way of the mysterious nature of the Real that brings in and takes away, that gives birth and dies unceasingly, so now only this great man's ashes remained, to be given to two great rivers, the Snake and the Gros Ventre. This latter was the same river in which we had scattered some of his dear mother's ashes, a little over two years earlier. Rhoda told us she had loved the mountain known locally as "The Sleeping Indian" (on Wyoming maps as Sheep Mountain) all her life. One Christmas we presented her with a large photo of this mountain, and she framed it to hang proudly on her living room wall. Given their intense emotional bond, I was not surprised to find that, like Jeff, her connections to the place prefigured his living there. Our sleepy little village of Kelly lay at the feet of "the Indian," and still-melting snow coursed from her broad bare chest down her craggy forested sides into the Gros Ventre, French for "big belly"—like Jeff!

To launch our afternoon's mission we (my son and his family, my step son, my niece and her boyfriend) decided to first stop in at Harvest Natural Foods for lunch. While there we ran into my friend Clarissa, who decided to join us for the Snake River portion of the ceremony, and to bring along another mutual friend, Rod, currently in remission from multiple myeloma, bone cancer.

We parked our cars near the entrance to Grand

Teton National Park and walked a short path down to the Snake, hauling the ashes in a backpack. We found a little spot on the river's edge somewhat clear of bushes, and not too treacherous for me to lean over the swirling currents, swollen grey with spring runoff—and I lifted out the heavy plastic sack from its golden can.

Without thought I decided that, rather than gingerly pour Jeff's ashes from the bag into the river, I would plunge my hands into his transformed mortal remains and cast the ashes into the air over the river, one handful at a time. The day was breezy; we all laughed as the ashes caught in the wind and returned to me; the slightly greasy, grey grit dusted my hands and drifted into my face and nose.

Clarissa told me afterward that my daughter-in-law Sue leaned in to say she had only attended one other ash-scattering, for Sean's father a year earlier, and that it had been a solemn occasion. "Oh, we don't treat death solemnly around here," Clarissa replied, standing next to Rod who grinned, seemingly at ease from a full year of meditating on mortality.

After scattering about a dozen handfuls, I stooped to wash my hands. When I stood up again I noticed ashes coating my Birkenstocks. "Hey, honey!" I laughed, lighthearted and insouciant, "You'll be with me always. I'll take you wherever I go!"

I still see faint grey traces on the black straps, and smile to remember that day.

It turned out that our time at the Snake was a dress rehearsal for the actual closing ceremony, several hours later, at the Gros Ventre.

We drove to the other side of the valley, where we planned to meet Ellen, another long-time friend, at her yurt; she would accompany us for the final scattering. I wanted to go to the spot on the river we call "The Greek

Isles" (a rocky promontory that reminds us of Greece), because that had been our destination on countless journeys. It's about a two-mile trek as the crow flies. But, Ellen reminded us, as usual in spring the log bridge over the little creek was swamped. She suggested we drive to the Gros Ventre campground and then walk upriver to the Greek Isles. But I resisted this idea. Jeff and I had never gone that way, and I wanted this final ritual to hold the memory of all those times we had wandered to that particular spot from our yurt in Kelly.

Instead, we decided bypass the creek and walk directly from Kelly to the river. We would take the longer path that curved along the river's edge, all the way to the Greek Isles.

Later several people said that we took exactly the right path, that this walk was the highlight of a most memorable day.

So there we were, traipsing single-file along the narrow path by the sun-sparkled, dancing river, with three-year-old Kiera setting a slow pace as she ran about, sniffing sage and grasses and stooping to look at rocks and insects alternating with holding up her arms for my stepson Trevor to carry her. We were walking in a long, ragged processional, the river's pace outstripping ours.

Held under a spacious blue sky, caressed by birdcalls, the soft swishing of the river, and a breeze shimmering newly opened bright green cottonwood and aspen leaves, the irreverence of the first part of this day's closing ceremony mutated, little by little, into silence. By the time we arrived at the Greek Isles our little band had sunk into reverie. Indeed, it seemed as if we had entered another zone entirely, and that the Snake and the Gros Ventre rivers had gifted us with two different moods of Jeff, one laughing and sacrilegious, and the other contemplative, silent and alone.

I decided to sit on the rocky promontory just where I had sat all those times he and I had come there to meditate. As ever, the little rock seat exactly fit my butt. Someone handed the can to me. I drew out the bag and sat there, for a moment, to center myself. Then I put my arm out over the river and poured some ashes into it, watched them drift into the rocks below and then slowly inch their way upstream, caught in an eddy. It was as if he was clinging to me. I needed to let him go.

I walked out to the tip of the promontory, where a four-foot standing wave had once risen each spring, until one year the river bent its course and flattened it. The current there was large and strong. I could let him go.

Once again I held my arm out, to release a small amount of the remaining ashes. (Why did I not pour all of them out at once? What held me back? It was not just he who clung.) I squinted into the sun gleaming on the river, wanting to trace the ashes' trail through the swift current until they disappeared. But, to my great surprise, after coursing a few feet, they somehow wandered back! How? Where was the countercurrent in this mighty flow? It did not seem possible.

Reaching out even further, careful not to tip myself in along with the ashes, I let a bit more go. And again! The ashes danced their way back, winking in the sun, eddying around my feet, seeming to defy "the physics of fluid flows." Again and again, I poured little bits out and they shimmied back. The others watched from above, stunned. Ellen remarked, "He's playing with you!"

Finally it was done. The ashes had vanished and I had rinsed out the bag. All this time, I had been descending deeper and deeper into myself. This day truly did feel like our personal closing ceremony, with me completing a chapter in my life, in our life, in his. A momentous occasion, this grand and poignant finale. I had to honor it more fully. How?

I turned to the others, and found them still staring, lost in thought. Suddenly, I needed desperately to be alone. Trying to compose myself so as not to seem abrupt, I suggested "casually" that they start back now, and I would catch up in a little while.

So the little ragged procession started back. I sat down in my meditation seat, waiting for them to be out of earshot and trying desperately to arrest the huge wave of sorrow building up inside me.

Aside from the vision of ashes dancing in the sparkling current, wending their way back to my feet, those next minutes are what I remember most from this closing ceremony. For as I sat there bursting with a standing wave of grief, my son Sean and his wife Sue stood directly above me with the children, adjusting straps on the sling for baby Drew. The moment was excruciating; I struggled to keep grief at bay while not swallowing it so completely that it would refuse to rise when called as they, oblivious to my plight, kept fussing with the straps. I wanted to scream, *Get out! Leave me alone*! but of course my experience of this grieving process was occurring in an entirely different universe from the one they inhabited. They had known Jeff on holidays. I had been joined to him body and soul. The gap between us in that moment was incommensurable, poignant.

Finally they moved off. I waited until I hoped they were out of earshot. Then, with a little coaxing, and counting on the river's hiss to further mask sound, finally the howls began. At first tentative and self-conscious, and then fused with the river's flow, body and soul's gut-wrenching agony flooded and released.

It never ceases to amaze me, when I do allow the expression of grief, that on the other side of that powerful, out-of-control turbulence I find peace. Tears, flowing in silence. We had surrendered to the inevitable. He was gone.

I sat there a few more minutes, reviewing scenes from past walks and meditations. The rising sun shining through the bush to my left as I sat in my rock seat on early September mornings. Winter's stiff, glistening snow cornices like whipped egg whites on the highlands to the south. The day when the newly weaned yearling moose followed me home, as if I were its mother; another day when I nearly stumbled on a newborn moose washed ashore from upriver while trying to cross with his mother during spring runoff—I hightailed it out of there before she arrived. The beavers who built their lodges up and down river so industriously and whose tail slaps on water I was sometimes privileged to witness; the squirrel who scampered up to sniff me, unafraid. The bald eagle who flew by, at eye height, on an evening river walk. All the hawks, ravens, bison, elk, deer, coyotes, even rumors of bears, from all the years. . . .

Finally I got up, glad for the space and time of reverie, intending to trail slowly behind them all the way back to Kelly.

I felt grateful and blessed for this respite, a rare pleasure on this journey with relatives and friends and responsibilities to Jeff's memory and mortal remains. But now it was done and I was glad, and sad, and above all relishing solitude, as I walked with head down, lost in thought—until I looked up, and there they were, waiting for me below a little bluff, only half a mile from where we had started back. I sighed to realize just how far apart we were, just how much grief over the loss of a primary partner separates one from others. And how much I, *right now*, needed that separation. And of course I loved them too, and felt supported by these dear people who were so concerned that they had waited patiently for me to rejoin them.

Our walk back was mostly silent too. We were a peaceful bunch; having meditated for two days on the mystery of impermanence, we were at one with his ashes flowing downriver to the sea.

I spent another five days in Jackson Hole, visiting with friends, walking around Jenny Lake at the foot of the Grand Teton, comparing haloes in a canoe on the oxbow of the Snake with my friend Jackie, also a new widow.

I was surprised to discover that our old stomping grounds did not trigger fresh grief. Perhaps this is due to the fact that I had lived in Jackson Hole for many years prior to Jeff's arrival, so that along with memories of us, I was unearthing memories of my self, alone. The return to Jackson helped me knit these lives together so that when I "think back" I do not stop with meeting him, but root further into my independent reality.

I continue to process Jeff's death, but at subtler levels. I remain connected to his two sisters, and especially to his father. We are talking about Thanksgiving in Massachusetts, along with my sons and Sean's little family.

Mid-July: the above paragraph, written a month ago, reeks with finality. But it's not true! My grief is *not* subtle; in fact it is just as strong, though longer and longer intervals separate its waves. For example, just the other day I was sitting in traffic, waiting for the light to turn so that I could continue to the county fair. I like to wander through the animal barns.

In recent years, I had asked Jeff to accompany me

on this annual pilgrimage—and he always did, reluctant but, as usual, willing to humor me. Once there he would try to get me to go on a carnival ride; I rode the Tilt-A-Whirl with him once, and nearly vomited. As I sat there in traffic, the memory of our times at the county fair triggered a strong wave of grief that I had sensed building for weeks. (Over and over again, I notice that engaging for the first time alone in an activity that we had enjoyed together triggers grief.)

I had barely enough time to roll up the windows before the howling began, eventually releasing tears. The light turned green. I kept one eye open to obey laws and make sure I didn't run into anybody, marveling at how expert I've become at splitting myself in two so that I can simultaneously both forcefully release grief and, meanwhile, continue in daily life. (I chuckled later at the thought of other drivers looking in my rolled-up window to see a woman with mouth stretched into a huge "O," eyes desolate and horror-stricken, driving along as if all was normal.)

I remain astonished at how grief and joy can simultaneously occupy the same space. And that as grief widens and deepens, so does joy. And how the embrace of both triggers an even more intense aliveness. Of course I "knew" this prior to Jeff's death—knew how paradox stretches boundaries so thin they collapse into oneness. I knew it in my mind, but I had not watched it happen inside myself—how the body fills and spills its grief; how then, at the very bottom of the trough (and the trough can seem immeasurably deep) the spark of life reignites, automatically, as spring follows winter, as day follows night.

Not until Jeff died could I even begin to embrace him fully. I find myself integrating certain of his interests—

his penchant for staying up late, his love for opera, and now, I find, even his email groups on esoteric subjects. Just last week I was invited to a local email discussion group, "Religion and Science," and it was not until after I had joined this mostly male company that I recognized it as exactly the kind of group Jeff had participated in. But me? Never—until now.

What other aspects of his seemingly endless being will I find myself incorporating? I stand bemused, beside myself, watching for clues.

Just yesterday I received a letter in the mail from Germany. A woman (whom I have never met) with great thoughtfulness sent me two photos of Jeff taken during his last trip to Europe (when he drafted the document setting up the non-profit status of the International Trager Association while mediating among the national Trager associations in their various languages).

In one of the photos, he is smiling in a manner both mirthful and sly. The look in his eyes startled me, it felt so deeply familiar and yet it was an aspect he had never actually shown me in life. I keep returning to that photo, noticing my gratitude (that she sent it), and my hurt (that he had not allowed me to see this quality in him). The photo shows just how very relaxed Jeff felt within Milton Trager's community.

The hurt dissipates when I acknowledge that it must have been easier for him to show his more personal self to a group of people who had a common focus (in this case, Trager bodywork) rather than to me, his intimate. That way his intensity could project into the group and be diluted through the Trager focus as intermediary. So I know he didn't mean to leave me out; it just felt too scary for him to deliberately reveal to me his more hidden, precious qualities. For I was The Other, standing directly across, unmediated and undiluted. With me, he was vulnerable. I could hurt him. And in my ignorance and relative lack of sensitivity, I did, at times, hurt him.

But, there he was again, in yet another community that drew out yet another aspect of his protean self! Another community that had comprehended another tiny sliver of his vast Being. What more will I learn about my dear "big guy" as the days and years roll on?

Each new discovery triggers further ruminations, altering memory, my comprehension of who we were together and why. In my daily tai chi practice I struggle to let go of thought, to fully inhabit my body right here and right now, so that I may make room for the Abiding Presence to sneak in and settle, to stay.

Until then, I hold the image of Jeff, appearing unexpectedly out of nowhere, as I opened the door to my son's home in Massachusetts on that sunny December day two weeks before he died. It was around noon. I saw him then as if for the first time, his large broad beaming face lit up like the sun. I intend to follow him now. Whether the years I have left on earth are many or few, I aim to dwell in that spaciousness natural to him as I leap from one of his giant footsteps to another, in sorrow and in joy, all the way home.

Part II

Our yurt in winter, Kelly, Wyoming.

*I*nterlude

Late June

I underwent my initial grieving process with an endpoint in mind: June 5, Jeff's memorial in Jackson, Wyoming, five months and one day from the day he died.

I didn't realize it then, but this period was a time capsule, sealed, with me inside it. I gave little attention to what lay beyond. So it should come as no surprise that when my plane from Jackson touched down in Indiana the capsule opened to reveal what I can only call existential dread.

Looking back, I now see Dread as the atmosphere attending the sudden shocked sensation that I was alone, traveling unimpeded and unnoticed in a vast and indifferent universe. The experience felt crushing; it reminds me of a student from "back east" who came to Idaho for the summer to "move pipe" in the flat, featureless wheat and potato fields near my hometown. The immense steel-blue bowl sky oppressed and terrified him. Within a few weeks he rushed back to the intimate, human-scaled hills and dales of New England.

Walking through the crowded airport, immersed in a silence so profound that I could hear my own breathing, I knew how that student felt. Where was I going? What was the goal? How could I even tell in what direction I was heading? And worse: who cares, what does it matter, given such immensity?

I was dimly aware of others bustling around me, but they seemed very far off, so inconsequential as to be nearly transparent. There was just me, just these lungs, filling space with monotonous mechanical whooshing.

My beloved companion had died, and I had drifted dreamily through five delicious and excruciating months, during which I hardly ever felt alone. I *wasn't* alone. I had been living in Jeff's generous and expansive aura. My initial grieving had to do with accepting, on all levels—on especially the visceral level—Jeff's altered status. And I was fascinated, the whole time, by the palpable resonance between us, the interdimensional pathways we seemed to be forging.

I was accustomed to the subtle, ongoing presence of Jeff's disincarnate self. Enveloped in his love, I felt real, sure of myself, clear. His illumination shone through my world, lending it color and weight and value. But now the memorial was over; it was time to move on. On the return flight I had meditated on the shift I needed to make. Admitting that I felt scared and unsure, I tried to convince myself to look forward.

But no matter how I tried to prepare, it seems that my mind was not capable of easing the way into my new reality. For suddenly, upon landing in Indianapolis, it was as if I had fallen from Earth into space. The sudden descent felt vertiginous, and the disconnect almost as intense as that First Night when I had hovered stiff as a board, suspended between heaven and earth.

Act One was over. Shock again announced Act Two, and it echoed the first beginning, in that its chief defining feature was Nothingness. Once again I found myself staring, from behind closed lids, into the Void.

Two weeks later, I grow accustomed to his routine absence—though punctuated with periodic check-ins. It's as if I am convalescent, and Jeff the doctor who pops in to check vital signs and monitor recovery. But he doesn't enter the room anymore; he just peeks in the door. And he seems in a hurry to move on. My soul wants to be generous, and gracious, and say, "Be well, my friend! Have a wonderful life!"—but my mind and body are not quite that far along. I have more grieving to do.

One night, recently, I woke up feeling a hand upon my heart, just as if a physical person were present, with open hand lightly resting on my chest. Was this Jeff? A few months ago I would have known it was he. Now I don't. And the gesture itself, though comforting, felt impersonal.

Yet, if I still need to grieve, why do I feel so alive? For if those first five months were yin, flowing and mysterious, then this second act feels decidedly yang, sharply active. Energy quickens, stirs inside. The "fire hose" spreads to include not just writing, but living.

The airport dread felt strong, but it was fleeting. I had a taste of what might come. Or perhaps not! For I feel so energized that already I have trouble invoking that disorienting sense of falling through space that had held me during the hour-long shuttle from Indianapolis to Bloomington. In fact I moved like a robot, deep in the dark of this strange malaise, until the moment when my key turned the lock on the door. Greeting me inside were not only my two cats, but a chipmunk, a mouse, a bird, and the sweet stink of what I discovered three days later was a long-dead bird—all brought in through the kitty-door.

Dread dropped me with a thunk, squarely into the mundane. I had things to do, immediately; I had reentered the structure built up over a lifetime to tame the Vastness into a tiny portion that I have learned to call my own.

Those initial months were also occupied with writing, my way of shaping and comprehending grief.

Another structure: this one just large enough to map the initial feeling process that his death set in motion. I imagine that I will stop this writing soon, around the six-month anniversary of his death. So again, what then?

Will Dread resurface? And if so, will I find the courage to consciously suffer that ill wind? Or will I scurry to bury panic in the minutiae of daily life?

I find it interesting that Dread, a subtle, almost metaphysical "feeling," came on so strong that it paralyzed thought and destroyed desire. Maybe Dread shouldn't be classified as a feeling, for when present, it seems so all-encompassing as to embody an alternate reality. In any case, I suspect that Dread lives on the other side of an invisible wall, kept in place by daily routines and the projective force of plans and projects.

Our culture tries to keep us "up." From childhood on, we are taught to build internal walls against any but happy feelings—as in, "I'm okay, you're okay" and, "Have a nice day." We are terrified of dropping into that netherworld where our conscious minds are useless and feelings of all kinds overwhelm us.

What we label as "depression" may signify a condition where we are dimly aware of the internal wall we unconsciously constructed to shield ourselves from the clamor of compressed (and therefore explosive) feelings. A wall that feels thick, solid, unmoving—crushing. In fact it doesn't feel like a wall at all, but like (what we imagine is, or may be) reality—the finality of our own personal death. Just the thought of death paralyzes us with fear; we feel suffocated, as if we are lying in a tomb, already dead and rotting.

Due to both cultural conditioning and our own fear of overwhelm, of course we want to avoid that particular awareness. So we pop Paxil, or Xanax or Prozac, or

Zoloft (I have heard that most therapists are themselves on antidepressants). Or we drink, or smoke, or eat, or shop, or make money, or buy a bigger car or house, or "entertain," or otherwise distract ourselves from what, we fear, is *not* there. Dread: the endless dizzying nauseating fall into a bottomless abyss.

I sense most of us have experienced Dread at least once—perhaps in a rare moment when, temporarily marooned, we suddenly and inexplicably dropped into the yawning space between carefully drawn lines. And yet I sense that if we dare to face Dread even momentarily, or for a few hours or days, we might learn that we don't fall off the world after all. At least that has been my experience.

As I learn to face and embrace Dread and other difficult psychological states, pharmaceutical "cures" for depression feel both inappropriate and unnecessary, in fact downright pernicious, in that they separate me from my own depths. I seek to engage the life of the soul and its evolutionary journey. I seek to continually return to and rebirth the vitality of my original nature. And I have a hunch that only as I embrace the troughs of despair will I also climb the peaks where joy resides.

If you have experienced depression, then you might argue that my experience of dread was so short as to not qualify as depression. But believe me, I have been there. In my early twenties as a young wife, mother and graduate student I moved like a robot, literally "bored stiff," so numb that there were times when I would suddenly, inexplicably, kiss my arm or pinch it just to make sure I was alive. Those years crawled by interminably despite an infernal busyness that covered an overwhelming, suffocating, barely suppressed panic that mocked my every effort.

So when Dread greeted me in the Indianapolis airport on June 12, it came as a sharp, short reminder of my own past. That Dread arrived with such suddenness, and in high contrast to the near-supernatural sense of security that I had enjoyed since Jeff's death, made the shock of it all the more profound.

On a more hopeful note, just as I have experienced the extremes of either suffocating solidity and/or nauseating emptiness *within* the phenomenon I call Dread, this supremely "negative" psychological condition, so have I on rare occasions, been plunged into a state of awareness *opposite to* the entire phenomenon of Dread itself.

I first tapped into this state one summer morning as a six-year-old. I was walking with my doll to my friend Edwina's house as usual, to play. What I remember is the sun's light and warmth, the green grass and trees, the deep blue sky, the slightly moving air. All this I had been aware of before, many times. But on this particular morning, somehow that awareness opened a door. All of a sudden, while walking along as usual, I dropped into another dimension, what I have since named "Abiding Presence." The ceaseless activity of the world and the constant churning of my thoughts all stopped; in their stead opened a timeless, spacious silence, holding everything in its embrace, as one.

If I may put that childhood experience in the context of the early history of western philosophy, it appears that I had stumbled into the Being of Parmenides, and discovered that it contains all of the Becoming of Heraclitus—every single drop of that famous river we can't step into twice.

It's interesting that Parmenides has not lived on in our cultural imagination as has Heraclitus. We view the ever-changing river of Heraclitus as a meditation on impermanence. His philosophy teaches us to let go of attachment to any particular experience (or person, or thing, or plan, or role, or education, or status, etc.). Heraclitus serves as a welcome counterbalance to the still-metastasizing busyness and materialism of western culture, where getting and having remain the measure of success.

However, when I meditate on the Being of Parmenides as well, I find it easier to let go of attachments, since while dwelling within the Abiding Presence my awareness feels at one with not just my own experiences but with the entire blooming world. For at least one bright and shining moment I do sense the miracle: all of creation is alive; the universe is shot through with awareness. In other words I need not fear impermanence, since to dwell within Being is to float in an ocean of endless abundance.

That first otherworldly experience of an all-pervasive luminous Presence remains as a tantalizing gift that shifted me, momentarily, into what I have since learned to recognize as "the Now."

But of course back then I couldn't hold it. In fact, while the experience startled and enticed, it also scared me. It felt so far outside the range of the normal that I had no words for it—and even now, over a half-century later, I have trouble describing this and other ineffable states. Indeed I am surprised that I can recall the experience, since for me language tends to encode memory.

It is interesting that my early flash into Oneness surfaces now, because I would say that my life during those first precious months after Jeff's death, when I felt embraced in Love, was exactly that: I had landed in the Abiding Presence, where Being and Becoming fuse into one.

So then, five months later, the landing at the airport: the fall from grace.

These two dimensions, Dread and the Abiding

Presence: is one the underbelly of the other? My friend Claudia claims that my experience of Love cushioned me from the eventual fall into the abyss that was bound to come next. That of course the dream world wouldn't last, for we encounter Dread as a natural part of the grieving process.

I don't want to believe her. I want to think I can just fall into the Love that so graciously accompanied his departure, then endure a mere flash of the abyss (making me ever more grateful for the Love), and then, finally, wake up again to normal life, washing my hands of grief. As in, "There. That's done! Now get on with it." In this desire I am thoroughly a product of my culture, wanting to get on with my business (my busyness) as soon as possible.

But I suspect Claudia knows what she's talking about. Over the nearly two decades of our friendship, this unusual woman has impressed me as the deepest psychological thinker I have ever known. In fact, were it not for her influence I might not be attending to or valuing this grief as a gift from the unconscious that subtly and continuously alters me as, bit by bit, it releases memories and their feelings to the surface.

I marvel at how, in the grieving process, the unconscious seems to give me exactly what I can handle at the time, no more and no less. Difficult memories surface only when I am ready for them, so that the more difficult the memory, the longer it takes to emerge. I am in awe of the natural wisdom of this seemingly regulated opening to the remembered past, and how it engenders a deep inner security—astonished that my own unconscious is so on my side!

Claudia's life path seems to be to restore value, both individually and culturally, to the life of feelings stored in the unconscious. When I first met her nearly two decades ago, I was split off from my feelings altogether; for the first few years, with unfailing empathy and patience, she nudged me to extract feeling from memory. This process invariably released ever deeper memories—and the feelings lodged in them—for review. In this way I learned to plunge into the depths, and to process old stuck emotions that had crippled me and prevented further unfoldment of my original nature.

Though Claudia and I live at great distance, we still periodically work with each other's "stuff" in long phone conversations. She helps me process my inner life, I help her realize how she is perceived by the outer world. After all these years under Claudia's tutelage, such deep internal work is almost (but not quite) natural for me, so that since Jeff's death I have been able to process grief, for the most part, on my own.

An exception is this characterization of Dread and Presence which, I decided, needed "the Claudia treatment." Here is her response: She thinks I have given Dread too big a role to play, that Dread is not on a par with Being (the Abiding Presence), but merely a reaction to not having plans, a temporary condition. But though I eventually find that she is usually right, I must stay with my own experience, in order to faithfully record what is true for me now. For me now, phenomenologically, Dread and Being are both states of awareness, approximately equal in magnitude.

Dread and the Abiding Presence as twins, even Siamese twins, joined at the head? Joined in my head. Which is which? They seem so much alike! Both lurk or reside beneath the surface of daily life and both seem to create and pervade space; both feel timeless and all-pervasive. Yet I sense them as opposites! In one I feel connected to everything and all's right with the world;

in the other only I exist, an infinitesimal dot sucked into a black hole. I have a hunch that which one I experience depends on my ego-state at the time.

In early childhood my ego was not yet fully formed, the boundary between me and the larger presence more like a membrane than a wall, permeable. Over the years, as I grew up, my ego strengthened to focus intent on plans and projects.

Then, at sixty years of age, the intense shock of discovering my husband's dead body on the bed popped me right through the wall—or it did, for a while. And on the other side of the wall was—Love! I was the child again, bathed in the warm waters of the universal womb—which however, ended five months later after Jeff's memorial.

As in Plato's famous myth, the seeker, having seen the sun, must return to the darkness of the cave. So on my return to Indiana from Jeff's memorial I had to re-enter *this* life on *this* earth, and was stunned to find myself utterly disoriented, valuing nothing over anything else, with no interest in plans and projects. That scared me, took my breath away. No longer a child whose ego was just forming, easily penetrated, I was adult: I *identified* with my ego and could sense nothing else. Just me, me alone, adrift in endless, suffocating space.

I am just now reminded of another time when I popped through the wall. Why do I remember this now? What is the nature of the thread I am following here? Yet I must follow it, else I ignore the subtly timed inner releasing of yet another memory that, apparently, bears on this discussion.

Why I am moved to continue to explore these rare and contrasting states of holistic awareness I'm not sure— and if it is all too much for you, dear reader, then please, simply skip to the next chapter. For in this particular chapter I do want to follow certain cues in the form of memories as they enter my mind. I intend to trail memory down.

This next, just-surfaced memory also involves a shocking change in the physical that popped me through the wall. That time it was not a radical shift in my husband's relationship to his body that sheared me from the ordinary, but a radical shift in my own body: an apparently mortal illness.

I was twenty-six years old, and for seven days had been lying feverish in Massachusetts General Hospital, my belly swollen with general abdominal peritonitis for which I had been given, one by one, over thirty intravenous antibiotics—all they had at the time. On the eighth morning, when the doctor came in he seemed discouraged; he checked my chart, then looked up, muttering, "I don't know what else to do for you."

I looked up, focused on his face. "Am I going to die?"

He seemed startled, even embarrassed. Then he shrugged his shoulders and hastily exited the room. (Imagine his discomfort, decades prior to Kubler-Ross, when a previously shy and introverted, extremely ill young woman dared to mention her own death.)

It was then that I made the single most important decision of my entire life: I chose to live rather than die. In doing so I made a deliberate, conscious decision to follow my own nature, wherever it might lead, intuitively knowing that this decision would alter my course forever.

This decision was not one that I'd known for a long time I needed to make, nor did it answer a rational question to which I had applied logic and the weighing of evidence. Regardless, illness finally pushed me over its edge. All of a sudden I heard a deep, booming internal voice.

The voice commanded, clear as day: *Live or die. It's your choice.*

Had this voice spoken to me when I was well and immersed in my usual busyness, I would have looked around to see who said that, and failing to find anyone, would have been terrified and wondered if I was crazy. But I was mortally ill, in an extreme situation—up against the wall—so to speak.

Did God speak to me during that decisive moment? Or did I "channel" a "spiritual guide"? Or, did my body's fever ignite an internal spiritual fire that suddenly popped through the wall, as a voice, into awareness? Whatever the source of the voice, the power of its command galvanized my entire body/mind onto an entirely new course.

In that one moment, I knew instantly and intuitively that I would live, and that in order to live I must "follow my own nature." However, I had no idea what my own nature was, indeed, I had not before applied the term "nature" to individual persons; nor did I, of course, know what it meant to "follow" my nature. Something through me or in me made that decision, something that knew much more than "I" did, something I would now associate somehow with "soul."

Needless to say, within twenty-four hours my belly had flattened and my fever had disappeared. My "spontaneous remission" surprised the doctors and affirmed the course I had just embarked upon. That morning, when I looked in a mirror, I was stunned to notice that the planes of my face had been rearranged.

I soon began to discover what following my nature meant. Just as a child learns the word "hot" when she touches a hot stove (in fact, "hot" was my first word as a toddler), so I began to learn from "mistakes" what was too hot to handle, what not. From the moment of my wake-up call in the hospital, I committed to learning primarily from personal experience—rather than from culture, tradition, books, other people's experiences codified into rules—and it was not exactly fun. In fact, deliberately setting out to learn from my own mistakes was (and sometimes still is) a messy, confusing, and often painful business. Indeed, early on, in this new life, sometimes my adventures were downright terrifying, full of drama and trauma—and not just for myself.

My heart still aches to recall what I put my loved ones through as, flailing blindly, I hunted down the scent of my own truth. For I knew intuitively that in order to follow my nature I had to move with what fascinated me, moment by moment—no matter how strange it might seem to others, or even to myself. If it truly fascinated me, it was mine to do.

I was running my whole life as if it was an experiment—as in, "Let's see, what will happen if I do this? Ouch!" Of course we all learn from our mistakes. This is the way we continually correct our courses. It's like sailing a boat; if we want to go in a certain direction, we need to sense the direction of the wind and then tack back and forth, always approximating, never quite true to the direction set. What made my case unusual was that, like a toddler but in full adulthood, I had deliberately chosen to learn from mistakes as my *primary* method of discovery about how both I and the world worked.

After a few years I finally did pause—to catch my breath, lick my wounds, and take stock. On the one hand, I knew that I had to keep going, that the only other choice was death (or depression: death in life). I had to continue to follow the current of my own life, no matter where it led, always assuming that whatever attracted me most was the next signpost along the way of my singular path.

Yet I was also highly aware of my own fear. In my nighttime dreams I walked unnoticed and unknown through vast and unfamiliar landscapes. In waking life I was flying in the face of tradition, of culture, of especially any residual "guilt" for my actions. (By this time I had identified "guilt" as our culture's glue, holding its members in place.)

At this juncture, to help me stay the course and remain true to myself, I adopted a personal motto. It was this: "Whatever I'm both fascinated by and afraid of, *that* is what I must do." And, in order to minimize pain—either to myself or others—I added a corollary: "Try not to make the same mistake twice," i.e., truly learn from each experience.

(You can rest assured that at no time, not even at the beginning of my quest, did I contemplate acting deliberately on murderous or otherwise harmful impulses. My intent was to disenculturate, not dehumanize, myself. Like Rousseau and Emerson and others in a long "romantic" tradition, I enjoy a gut sense that human beings, when allowed their own natural development, are inherently good.)

I am happy to report that after about fourteen years the drama did begin to subside. My "mistakes" created a body of knowledge that I could draw upon in reflection. I began to sift through significant memories, both to recognize how actions create consequences, and (thank you, Claudia) to recognize and honor the feelings buried in those memories. As a natural result of this long and intensive reflective process, I began to have compassion for my own struggle and to commit myself to healing certain relationships, especially those with my parents and my own children.

My learning process grew more efficient and refined. I didn't have to repeat myself so much—at least not in small ways. For as I grew older I began to gain more of a bird's-eye view, and discovered that some repetitions involve large patterns that play themselves out over a span of years, even decades, and I began to see how they all combine to form the larger trajectory of my life.

Thus as I grew older my discoveries about myself grew richer, deeper, and more complex. Each time I recognized a pattern that played itself out over a long time span, I felt tremendously excited. What a eureka moment! For, I knew I had a chance to release the pattern, once detected. Of course, it would take time and effort to do so, since locked in any pattern was a compressed, complex knot of feelings that required much patience and subtlety to discern, unravel, re-experience, and finally release. Each release of feelings and the pattern that had boxed them freed me to live more in the moment. In this way, my world gradually became more and more interesting. Like a curious child, I felt thrilled to be alive.

As larger and larger patterns started to clear up and out, I began to pay attention to what was happening while it was happening, rather than later, when it was too late and I had created yet another hurtful mess which involved not only myself but other people. In other words, I began to detach myself from total identification with my own ego, to "lighten up" and develop a sense of humor. And I was beginning to create a "fair witness" to my experiences. This light of awareness, at first rare and intermittent, has grown to become, as I begin my 7th decade, a near-constant steady illumination, a beacon that lights the way out of whatever dark tunnel I encounter—including the death of my beloved husband.

Lest you think that I was graced with courage or

luck to have attempted such an extreme course and yet emerge relatively unscathed, please realize that many times during those early years, in order to drum up my nerve, I would repeat my motto endlessly, like a mantra: "This fascinates me. This is what I'm afraid of. This I must do!" It had worked so far; I was counting on it working again. And it always did. I was learning much more by focusing on what both fascinated and frightened me than I would have learned had I stuck with the tried and true. My life has been one long continuous opening.

Which brings me to the present. Now, nearly four decades later at sixty, I stand at yet another crossroads. In order to follow my nature through the grieving process over my husband's death I must repeat the current variation on my personal mantra, developed in order to process grief: "Whatever feeling threatens to overwhelm me, *that* is what I must allow."

Just now the feeling that overwhelms me is confusion. I sense that I do not comprehend much of what I am trying to discuss here, that I am a fool if I think I do. And that, years later, maybe even two weeks from now, I will want to erase this entire discussion as hopelessly muddled.

I could call my muddle a mutant form of Dread. For, as usual, being a dramatic person, I leap from part to whole: "I don't understand anything!" Once again, the bottom falls out and I tumble through the Void.

So, Dread. Yes. I must admit: it is the abyss itself, which fascinates—and always has. Indeed, I have hiked in mountains all my life, and have yet to meet a cliff face that I haven't been tempted to step off, thinking maybe I could fly.

So, Dread. Dread could be the monster blocking the shining path ahead. I want to learn to become accustomed to Dread, to invite Dread in, to relish how it clears the decks, its delighted dance with impermanence.

Dread may be one gate into the Mystery. Yet I sense that, given my nature, I will never dwell within Dread at length—at least not consciously, not with awareness. For as a Sagittarian, I have been gifted from birth with an abundance of fiery energy, and I am temperamentally an eternal (or foolish) optimist. It is difficult for me to even get to the place where my plans and projects do not fill me with excitement as I rise to their challenge.

But what about those moments when expectations come to naught and the bottom drops out? Is Dread liable to steal in? Once again, I may be caught in the horror of impermanence, which as before, I must resolve to face and fully embrace.

And if I am fortunate, perhaps in time I will, without having to go through Dread, be gifted with the capacity—or better, through daily meditative practices, I will actually develop the skill—to shift *at will* into the mysterious Abiding Presence, that all-encompassing seamless Love that Jeff and my entire community called upon, in the early stages of my grief, to ease my way forward without him.

What I Didn't Want to Tell You

October

    I didn't want to tell this story—didn't want to even think the experience was something that "happened" to me. But now, after more than a month of being stopped, indeed stuck, I realize that ignoring it blocks not only my writing, but my being. So here is the story, in a nutshell.

    There was someone else. While I was grieving for Jeff. During a certain three-month period.

    I have already written about two of those three months. So the tale I told is a partial truth. At the time, this other story seemed alien to my grief; I couldn't stomach the idea of telling it.

    The other relationship has been over for a while. Long enough for me to realize that the truth is not complicated after all. From the vantage point of nine months I see that all my experiences have been aspects of my grieving process, and the "other man" theme a particularly potent current within it.

    During those dramatic three months, however, it did seem as if both relationships were going on, and with equal intensity. At first I tried to ignore Peter's presence, because any connection with him felt disloyal to Jeff—my memories of Jeff, my grief, his continued out-of-body presence in my life. But it happened. Peter did exist. At least I think he did. But he wasn't "real" either. I never saw his body, never touched him, felt him. In truth, for a short while there, I was in a tense but hilarious triangle with two men, both of whom existed only in my mind.

If neither of these men were "physical," at least to me, then why am I filled with shame and embarrassment when I recall the story?

I think I'm now beginning to fathom what was going on.

The Peter Connection began the day after my ceremony to clear the basement of the emotional residue from Jeff's books. If you recall, I woke up feeling terrible the day after Dean drove off in the loaded U-Haul. I had hardly slept, and rigid staring and staticky nerves had marked my night, nearly as bad as the first night after Jeff died.

The contrast between waking up the day after Dean left and waking up the following day after the clearing ceremony, startled me. I felt newborn, and greeted the dawn like an old returning friend.

Energized and thrilled to be alive, I sat down to check my email. And there it was, the message that was to change my life. So I soon thought.

The letter was from a man with whom I had been in contact years before when he had emailed to say how much he enjoyed an essay of mine, originally published in a book in Holland, that he had found on the Internet. That email had stood out, partly because I was surprised to learn the essay was on the Internet, but mainly because the man lived in Sweden. I was thrilled to think that someone from so far away appreciated my work.

I had shown the original letter from this "Peter" to Jeff. The three of us enjoyed a brief email exchange, details of which I don't remember. But, a few months ago, during the time I was corresponding with Peter, I looked back on that earlier occasion to notice how quickly I had included Jeff in the dialogue. Did I sense even then that this man would come to rival Jeff for my attention? Indeed, I remembered looking at his very name, Peter Lundgren (I have changed it here slightly, to protect his privacy), with a sudden, though subtle sense of longing—which, being married and innately loyal, I quickly squashed.

So now I was hearing from Peter again, and again, it was because of something I had written. In February, I had emailed the chapter "Phenomena" to a number of people. Perhaps he was on a list of mine. At any rate, he wrote saying he was in New York and would read "Phenomena" when he got home. At the time, this email barely registered. Jeff had recently died and, looking back, I would say I was in a state of suspended animation, cushioned in a cloud—that sometimes felt like cloud nine, and other times like sedation.

Fast-forward a few months, to that day when I woke up feeling reborn after clearing the basement. Peter had written again, having finally read "Phenomena." This email was long and amazingly heartfelt to be coming from a near stranger. He began by giving me his astrological birth information—which is unusual. What stranger tells me this, unless I ask? Or unless he or she wants to consult with me as an astrologer?

He then plunged into his own life, saying how struck he was by the fact that his girlfriend of ten years had left him on January 5, only one day after Jeff died. He told me many things about himself—his profession, tales from his childhood, some of his views on life. He ended with an apology for bothering me with this kind of letter, which he knew was totally inappropriate to send to someone whose husband had just died, but "something in the way you write makes me bubble forth about myself."

That letter got my attention. This was the end of

April. I was almost four months into my grieving, and the fog of shock was lifting. The coincidence of dates surrounding Jeff's death and his girlfriend's departure startled me, especially in view of the fact that his email had arrived on the morning I was feeling reborn! The timing of the two dates felt auspicious; I have long been attuned to coincidence, and it seemed I was being alerted to a path I was meant to follow.

I set up Peter's birth chart, and discovered that his 23° Scorpio Ascendant and 25° Scorpio Moon were directly opposite my own 23° Taurus Moon.

That astrological link instantly triggered an even deeper attachment. It was as if I had suddenly opened the door to a room I had no idea existed, but which a part of me knew had been there all along. And my Moon—site of forever unfulfilled childhood needs and longings—was involved!.

I should have known that this kind of a connection might be suspect, since I am no longer a child. However, as an adult I have encouraged my timid-inner child self to become more spontaneous. And, given my metaphysical world-view which includes dimensions and energies not visible to the eye, for decades now I have been alert to meaning found in the timing of events, and I notice synchronicities as signposts along the way. The unusual combination of our Moon-alignment and the timing of the two dates activated an ancient internal homing device forever seeking its target. Peter was it. My New Man.

As Jeff exits, so Peter enters. Of course! Nature abhors a vacuum. New life rushes in to fill it.

But no! I thought. That's impossible! It can't be! I am deeply in grief. Can't let myself be sidetracked by anything, especially a new relationship!

Contradictory feelings were flooding in: on the one

hand, there was my grieving process, a long slow letting go that, unbeknownst to me then, had only barely begun; on the other hand there was the miraculous timing of this sudden connection!

The reborn me felt ecstatic, turned on, as if my finger had been plugged into a light socket. The rest of me was, as ever, surrendered to the dark cave of grief.

I was pulled in two directions. Both felt real, though mutually exclusive. The grieving part of me was appalled at my sudden excitement.

This explosive stretching occurred in the space of a few minutes. I couldn't stand it, couldn't hold the inner contradiction without bursting. It was all too much. I wrote Peter back to say that, according to both timing and our astrology, there was an incredible connection between us, but that I would have to ignore it as "completely inappropriate for this time in my life." Now I ask myself why I mentioned the "incredible connection" between us, if I wanted to ignore it?

He wrote back, apologized again, then asked that I at least send him other chapters as I wrote them.

I agreed to this, and in a softer tone said he could respond to each new one as I wrote it, because I would appreciate his feedback. But, I sternly demanded, just one letter in response to each piece! No exchanging emails!

This did little to quench the sudden flare-up of feelings alien to those I had been working with. For the flame, once kindled, did not die out. And telling him of our connection was my unconscious way to ensure that he not go away.

I was trying to have my cake and eat it. Wanting to be the "pure new widow" and meanwhile hold out the possibility of a new connection to replace the one just lost.

As if I could ever "replace" Jeff! As if that rich and

mysterious, memory-filled connection, the deep running trust between us, was a mere commodity.

In fairness to myself, I was not really serious about replacing Jeff. Had I stopped to consider it, I would have said that was impossible: Jeff cannot be replaced. He was an utterly unique being, as was his presence in my life. However, back then I was still in the initial stages of my grieving process, and replacing Jeff was exactly what I had in mind. Only now do I begin to fathom why.

In the early months after Jeff died, it seemed that I was immersed in his aura, surrendered to Love. It took time for me to separate out enough to recognize how desolate I actually felt. Our partnership had been the given. Everything else revolved around it. After twelve years, I had so taken our mutuality for granted that I had no idea the extent to which unplugging from Jeff would leave a gaping hole in me.

After nine months I finally begin to acknowledge that hole, to gingerly probe its yawning depth. My hope is that, given time, I will be able to absorb and integrate irreparable loss.

In those early months, the fog (and Jeff's felt presence) cushioned me from feelings that, had I been able to access them, would have overwhelmed me. Mercifully, the unconscious does only seem to divulge as much as I can handle at any particular time, with the remainder still buried—or appearing in disguise. So yes, back then, there was a part of me that did want to "replace" Jeff to avoid unrecognized pain.

This, I think, is the key to what was going on. It is the key to my shame (that I should even *think* about replacing Jeff so soon, and that I would assume Jeff *could* be replaced) and it is the key to my embarrassment (I *still* want to be the pure new widow!). Furthermore, it is the key to the fact that the short-lived bond with Peter was a false but instant and tempting substitute for my relationship with Jeff.

I was used to being in relationship. Suddenly losing my mate had left me dangling.

Many people go through this experience, of course, and some bounce from one person to another, whether or not the partner has just died. We call it the rebound effect, and volumes have been written on this usually ill-advised practice. In my case, once the Peter connection was over I felt embarrassed and even disgusted to realize that, just like other people, I had succumbed to bewitchment during my grieving process.

Looking at my embarrassment now, I realize it has to do with ego. I had thought myself different, special. By inviting all feelings in and working with them, I thought I would work with grief in a new, more conscious way, and then, in my usual teacher role, pass on my hard-earned wisdom to others! Peter was my Waterloo, and I thank him. For if I truly do want to be conscious, then what needs my attention is the hard stuff. And this three-month period, and its aftermath, was decidedly hard.

As I wrote the next several chapters I sent them on to Peter. He responded with more tidbits about himself. Now I can see we were leading each other on; then I thought that while it was odd he didn't say much about my writing, I was glad to learn more about him.

Not even two weeks went by before I abruptly changed course. I dropped my "terms" for our correspondence, saying it wasn't fair to him because I was trying to control the situation, and that didn't feel good to me.

This change of heart was triggered by a waking dream early one morning—as I arose from sleep, a vision of three dolphins swimming together in the sea. This vision shifted my either/or paralysis into both/and: the three of us—Jeff, Peter and me—as members of the same pod. I assumed Jeff, for whom Dolphin had been the primary totem animal, had sent the vision.

Well, that shift released a flood of emails back and forth, often many times a day. Peter and I discussed our lives, our histories, things we liked and disliked; we compared and analyzed social and political conditions in the U.S. and Sweden. And he told me about his financial difficulties (having quit his thirty-year salaried position two years before, he was still learning the psychology of successful self-employment).

In response to his evident distress I switched to my default mode, that of "counselor." (Jeff had adamantly refused this part of me, which forced me to drop the pretense of objectivity—or is it superiority? But few men resist it so directly.)

Peter and I looked forward to our emails so much that we told each other they were the best part of our day. And it was true! I loved his mind (as I loved Jeff's mind; perhaps my only necessary criterion for a man is that he be extremely intelligent), and I relished the fact that he truly seemed to like to discuss things with me (unlike Jeff, who was taciturn and introverted). Peter was full of interesting ideas on many subjects. I could learn from him! (His wide-ranging curiosity also reminded me of Jeff.)

Meanwhile, of course, the undertow of grief was always there, dragging me down, making me feel resentful and then, when I noticed my resentment, guilty. I loved the Peter "high." Each morning I eagerly arose to sit at my computer for that morning's greeting from Sweden. Those few days when I didn't get one felt devastating.

Peter had become my lifeline. That he was there for

me seemed to offer a new plan.

During those three months my future seemed clear, or at least possibly so; now that he too has gone, the future feels vague, ill defined. I was using the relationship with Peter to mask the uncertainty and anxiety that Jeff's death naturally precipitated.

I am not surprised that I attracted Peter to me during the initial phases of the long, slow loosening of grief's grip; for so distinctly uncomfortable is this awareness of not knowing where I am going that, had Peter not appeared on the horizon, most likely I would have conjured up someone else. In my wiser moments I know that not knowing is the human condition; however, like most, I normally live inside an illusion that I do know what lies ahead.

Back then, that I would get so upset over so small a matter as not seeing an expected email from him upset me further. I castigated myself for already fixating on this man as a replacement for Jeff, and was disgusted with my obsessive neediness. In fact, my extreme emotional reactions to whether-or-not-I-heard-from-Peter-that-day set off internal alarm bells and made me wonder about my mental and emotional state. Yet I tried to squash the nagging doubts.

Even more troubling, it seemed to me that Jeff was also upset. I assumed Jeff had sent Peter to distract me so that Jeff could disentangle from my need for him and go on. Was this wishful thinking? A way to quell anxiety, to smooth things over? Or was it real? Did the vision of three dolphins really come from Jeff?

That had been a powerful vision. But what if it wasn't real? Then what was real? How could I trust any of my perceptions? What if the new lifeline wasn't real either?

From my current perspective, I have no idea which

of my internal imaginings back then had actual correlates in the world beyond. Inner and outer had collapsed. There was no way to differentiate between them, and no need to. I was surrendered to Oneness. But now the fog is gone. I look back and see a woman for whom the boundaries between worlds seemed to thin and disappear, a woman who apparently sensed things of which I am no longer in touch. Either that, or I was kidding myself—all along, or just in matters relating to Peter.

In any case, whatever my internal condition back then, as the email romance heated up I did seem to sense that Jeff was both startled and annoyed by the alacrity with which I had taken up his offer in the dolphin dream. (Or, was *Jeff is upset* a projection of a startled and annoyed part of myself?)

I told Peter this, and that's when it really felt like I was in a triangular tug-of-war with two invisible men. Is it to be Peter or Jeff? It can't be Peter, because Jeff is still there. But Peter came in at such a propitious time! And Jeff sent him to me! But Jeff's upset with this turn of events, he knows it's unseemly, utterly inappropriate. So do I. Even Peter has raised doubts about this connection starting up so soon.

But such was the strength of my daily euphoria in our email exchange that I was hooked, addicted, and not about to let go.

Meanwhile there were final preparations to make for the Jackson memorial. Every time I talked with anyone about Jeff and the memorial and my grief—especially when I talked with someone from my family or his—I felt like a hypocrite. I was telling them my truth, and yet, since I never mentioned Peter, not my whole truth. I did speak of Peter to my sons, and to several close friends, whom I swore to secrecy. All seemed to be much more understanding of the situation than I. But now I wonder what they were really thinking.

In any case, I was quite capable of dropping down into the grieving-Jeff mode, once I'd had my daily Peter fix. We originally connected at the end of April. A hundred emails later it was the end of May, time to leave for Jackson and the June 5th memorial. Weeks earlier I had informed Peter that I didn't want us to begin talking on the phone until after the memorial. The idea of hearing his voice seemed so much more personal; I could at least observe this discretion.

In my shame, I was hiding him.

Furthermore, I told him not to expect any emails from me during my twelve days away, as I needed to move fully into the long-planned family and community ceremony to celebrate Jeff's life.

I was determined to keep the two worlds separate, not to "contaminate" the primary one with the other.

At first, while in Jackson, I still felt like a hypocrite, so much was Peter on my mind. But as time went on I gradually surrendered to that environment. By the day of the memorial itself and over the days following, full of heartwarming Jeff stories in visits with old friends and family, "Peter" began to seem like an abstraction. In fact when I finally returned to Bloomington and opened my email, I hesitated before writing him, and when I did, just said, "I'm home. Are you still there?"

His response—"Of course!"—was so swift and reassuring that, all at once, there it was again! The connection! I had nearly forgotten about it, nearly let it go. Only hazy tendrils linked us before those two little words thundered back, and once again I was plunged into the emotional soup that had felt so nourishing before and, I apparently, still needed. The tiny part of my awareness that still had its head above water did wonder at the time: Do I really want to do this? But even that was banished as the Moon's undertow dragged me by the hair into its lair.

Now we were talking on the phone. Lots of ideas, thick and fast, about lots of subjects. But more and more now Peter talked about being exhausted, even depressed. Every morning he was having trouble just getting out of bed.

Looking back, I realize he probably felt used. At first he had told me I was giving him energy. Then, during those weeks in Jackson when I forbade all communication, I took energy away.

I still needed to be in control. Being the new widow gave me that control, automatically. All I had to do was invoke it.

I had taken energy away, which left him feeling disempowered—not helpful for someone in chronic, economic survival mode. His increasing vulnerability scared me, made me want to take control even more so I could fix him, make him better.

Now I realize that most of our communication in what turned out to be the final phase of our relationship concerned the fading state of his mental and emotional health. Not only did he not make enough money to pay current bills, he was riddled with debt and at times, while waiting for a check, reduced to picking berries to avoid starvation. As his counselor, I desperately urged him to shift perspective so his real-world conditions could shift. Yet, of course, his situation was beginning to infect me, drag me down.

I felt guilty that, thanks to Jeff's legacy, I didn't share Peter's poverty. A part of me wanted to help him financially, and I even made a few tentative remarks in that direction. But he ignored them. Even then, I knew it was good he did. It meant he wasn't trying to use me.

I was beginning to lament his lack of chi, the fact that he had no energy, and to contrast that with my own energy, which, thanks to daily tai chi and chi kung practice, remained high, despite my grief. (*Of course* I tried to convince him to learn tai chi.)

I began to distance myself by viewing him as an archetype: I wondered why I had attracted someone like Peter, and to compare him to other men in my life who had also been depressed, seemingly stuck in situations with no way out. (Jeff fell into that category when I met him.)

Duh! I think now. I attract depressed men because my unconscious continues to bring up old childhood trauma. It was World War II; my father was overseas and my mother felt terrified her husband would never return. Peter's (and Jeff's, and certain other men's) depression echoes that of my mother back then. And my behavior with Peter (and the rest of them, except for Jeff: thank God he refused!) echoes what she tells me I used to do as a two-year-old: sing and dance to make her happy.

Her depression left me feeling emotionally abandoned. Yet she was still my mother; I was in communion with her, breathing her aura night and day. I was both sad and anxious at being abandoned, and I had absorbed *her* depression.

In trying to make Peter happy, the little girl in me was still trying to make my mother happy so she could mother me. Through my familiar and comfortable role of counselor I have masked my own underlying, and still apparently unhealed depression.

I was replaying that old emotional pattern of abandonment. It was a pattern Jeff and I had recognized; among other aspects of his being, Jeff was very nourishing, a wonderful mother. His departure left that child in me suddenly bereft, triggering the old pattern during the time when I was plunged into grief. Was I, I ask now, projecting my depression onto Peter, so that instead of facing it in myself I could help him with his? Now that I think about it, it seems obvious.

So yes, I aim to invite all feelings in, and to work with them in myself, rather than project them onto others. But I begin to recognize that the most difficult feelings are also the most difficult to directly access. So dominant is the unconscious, that in the split second before these feelings can rise into awareness, they get projected.

There are so many, many layers to the psyche! I have long known this, but whenever something happens that, despite my determined attempts at understanding, completely flummoxes me, I am left once again in awe over the astonishing creativity of the unconscious, how it dreams up situations to present me with lessons I need while itself remaining unrecognized.

I made a decision decades ago to continuously seek to dissolve ego and access inner truth, to be as honest as possible about what is really going on. Seeing the lengths to which my ego still goes to stay "on top" of things, I am again forced to bow before the intricate complexity of the dance of experience, and what seems to be the impossibility of always immediately recognizing what is real and current and what a mere replay of a past scene.

The rest of the tale is predictable. Peter finally called a halt to our "relationship," saying he just didn't have the energy to continue. True enough. Right away, though I was of course, stunned by his sudden announcement, I knew this decision appropriate. And even then I had the presence of mind to look back and be amazed at my own behavior: I knew of his lack of energy all along! But so addicted was I to his (my) depression that I was blinded to the unsustainability of the relationship.

He told me this in early August, ten days prior to the trip I had planned to see him. By this time, though we were still frenetically emailing, our relationship had already cooled to that of "just friends," so the shock was not as great as it might have been. After a few days of frantically looking at options I decided to take the trip anyway, and was lucky enough to slide into a Scandinavian tour group at the last minute.

The stronger shock, since it so perfectly echoed my abandonment as a child, had come a month earlier—just after I booked tickets for the trip—when Peter emailed to say "I am falling deeply in love with a woman, and this woman is not you." Just like that! One might think him cruel for announcing this so abruptly, with seemingly no consideration for my feelings, but I think his statement reflects the fact that he was as surprised as I. He was saying that it could have been me, but wasn't.

He said he had met her (again via email, she lives in Canada!) during the time I was in Jackson. Of course I was amazed and puzzled that he would "fall for" another virtual relationship just after I had committed to see him in person. I imagine that, given his own grief and depression, he needed to avoid our face-to-face encounter.

I now see the coincidences that propelled me into the Peter connection as indeed meaningful—just not in the way I expected. Peter and I were meant for each other, in the sense that our separate trajectories propelled us into a meeting of minds and hearts during a period when we would mirror each other's lunar needs and avoidances. I thank him for his disclosure about another woman, for it instantly triggered my Moon's old abandonment so fully that I was plunged into re-experiencing it. Indeed, I'll never forget that awful muggy July day when I plugged directly into loneliness and worthlessness, dragged down by hopelessness. The day went on forever. I lay immobilized, deep inside my own darkness, trapped in despair.

That night I fell ill, and for the next forty-eight hours my mind was submerged inside a flu-wracked body, as my whole being worked to integrate mental and emotional shock.

But that was it! The next day I was fine.

I realize that three days is not very long to process sudden loss, and certainly three days is not nearly long enough to qualify as "depressed." On the other hand, I am sixty years old and have been doing this kind of emotional work for decades. Moreover, I like to think that this work has borne fruit.

When I was in my early twenties, as a mother with young children, I was living out my mother's life—and hating it. The old unrecognized wound manifested in my maternal behavior: as she couldn't mother me during a crucial developmental time, so I was unable to mother my two little boys—in the sense that mothering did not feel natural. I felt like I was a fake, pretending. In my late twenties I broke free of both marriage and motherhood, and ran to catch up with *my* life. I sought extreme experiences, frantically grasping for intense highs to stave off equally intense lows.

In my forties, the fast life unraveled. My body started to rebel, and somehow I was graced with the capacity to turn around and slow down. Thanks to Alice Miller's *The Drama of the Gifted Child*, I began to work deliberately with my "inner child," both in my journal and in conversations with treasured female friends also on this path of processing difficult experiences rather than trying to ignore or deny or project them.

Whenever I felt upset or depressed I would ask myself what had triggered it, and why had I invited that experience in? In this way I attempted to take responsibility for my life, by working with whatever had currently triggered and illuminated an otherwise unrecognized part of myself. Usually this meant: what old childhood drama was I re-enacting? And how can I heal the inner child so that she won't need to constantly retrigger, in present circumstances, the repeating trauma of old wounds?

In this way I began to cultivate awareness. However, even though I was openly enduring what I had run from before, the experience was so painful that I spent long months, and sometimes years, in a druggy, lethargic state, medicating with marijuana to push away the awareness and to dull the sharp ache of solar plexus pain.

By the time I was in my fifties I was capable of working through an old emotional replay in months; at fifty-five, it took weeks. Now, at sixty, this replay took just a few days, its extreme brevity no doubt due to the fact that ours was a virtual relationship: my body and aura had not tangled with Peter's.

I began this inner work two decades ago. I am encouraged that, though with each return of old karma the feelings that come up are every bit as intense, the time span during which I re-experience them continues to shorten.

I recognize this inner evolution as a gradually strengthening center of awareness (I have not studied Buddhism, but I suspect it is akin to what Buddhists call "mindfulness"). For, during that one long depressed hot July day when I processed the shock of "losing" (the illusion of having) Peter, I not only felt lost and abandoned, I was also highly aware of feeling that way. The aware part of me was witnessing my emotional devastation in a detached, dispassionate, and even, yes, curious and compassionate manner.

It may sound odd to speak of curiosity and

compassion in this context, and it felt odd, too, at the time. But perhaps that's because conscious juxtapositioning of different parts of the self does feel odd when we are not accustomed to it.

I am grateful to Peter for partnering with me in this three-month learning process. The timing was propitious. I was gifted with the opportunity to re-experience, in a remarkably short period, a cycle that involved what is perhaps my oldest, most primal emotional wound. The wound that was re-activated, though unrecognized, with Jeff's death.

So, in the end, I look upon the Peter connection as a cautionary tale for myself. I now realize that, given the gaping hole in my emotional being, I am vulnerable to relationship during this period of mourning. And I realize that even if a man came into my life who truly was appropriate, I might not recognize him, so blinded am I by projections.

I am now forced to admit that grief is a natural process that follows its own laws. Grief is way bigger than my conscious understanding of it. I will have to go through it until it is done.

Yet, even now my conscious mind wants to control events, to ask, "How will I know when it's done?" And my response is, I don't know. I don't know how I will know. If it is at all like other experiences in my life, it will not be a matter of knowing at all, but of feeling. One day I shall just wake up and it will be done.

Or maybe not. Maybe I will learn that this kind of grief is never done, that the loss of my beloved truly is irrevocable. No one can replace him. No one. And that even so, somehow, someday, I will be able to go on anyway, with relative equanimity and in relative wholeness.

Meanwhile, I must allow this process to take me

where it wants to go. For the truth is, as long as I am in grief I am in the grip of a mighty power that supercedes my more mundane mind. I need to put all but the most immediate plans on hold, to move into the moment, and endeavor to stay there.

Thanks to Jeff's estate, I am in the enviable position of having my physical needs taken care of, so that I can move down into grief without having to worry about how I will support myself, or go to work every day at some kind of demanding job. I feel for those who lack time or opportunity, whose survival needs must take precedence over their inner lives. Because I am going through this process and it seems so rich to me, I cannot imagine how people can process grief any other way. But of course, they do, because the most interior part of them must. Each person works with grief somehow, in some way, to some extent.

Some, like myself, need solitude and quiet; it is unfortunate that only a few are blessed with the choice to stop everything and give themselves to this process for the unforeseeable future. For others, continuing to work as usual helps them through their grief. As I notice myself carving my day into ordered segments, so I imagine the discipline of going to work each day helps them manage the emotional chaos attending loss.

In the past, widows often wore black to signify that they were, for the time being, set apart from ordinary life. There was more cultural support for grieving as a natural process. Now our culture is so frenetically busy; we seem to have lost trust in our ability to find our own internal resources to work through grief.

I'm worried about the trend in our society that attempts to dominate this process for the benefit of a seemingly monolithic cultural machine that has so much momentum that even our private lives are sucked up into it. Now, when we supposedly, thanks to machines, have more time, we medicate people so that they can continue to produce and to consume. Not very long ago, when medications were not so ubiquitous and only a few people were medicated, most people had to work through their grief rather than short-circuit it. And it was accepted that their functioning would be, for a time, impaired.

Now we try to streamline grief, often relegating it to a counselor, and allow it a certain timing. In this way a natural process has been subjugated to the economy. Everybody's caught in the same squeeze. Insurance payouts for grief counseling are limited, which encourages counselors to prescribe drugs as a therapeutic short-cut. And people want the drugs, of course, to support them in "getting up to speed" as soon as possible so they don't "lose their competitive edge"—or, more starkly, to get that paycheck in order to survive.

Underneath this economic bottom line, however, I sense there may lurk a deeper motivation: our shared terror of touching the actuality of all the grief. And there's a truth to that. The fear of getting stuck, bogged down, of engulfment, of never coming back, is real. In rare instances, it does happen. And there is also the shared process, how our particular culture tends to constrict even private emotion. And there's the shared necessity to be able to continue, to not stop, through enormous grief.

I do wonder if, below the often noticed loneliness attending our mass conditioning into celebrated American values of "independence," "freedom," and "self-reliance," there is also this silent shared suffering. And I would not be surprised if most people are secretly depressed, in grief.

For it appears that in our rush for the next best thing we have just about forgotten the inner world, home not just for depression but for the creative spirit that, I am discovering, given any chance at all will reveal its divine, miraculous capacity to heal, to make us whole.

I remain, secure and protected, with our two kitties, in the sweet little house Jeff bought before we moved here. Large maple trees canopy the roof and yard. I enjoy working with my hands, in the kitchen and in the garden and in fashioning vessels from clay. My house sports two new doors—doors with windows—which I have painted a bright blue. I continue to work with watercolor and each time I complete a painting that pleases me I feel a twinge of pain that I can't show it to Jeff.

I continue to reparent myself by creating my own little nest so that the needy part of me will finally settle down and know that my adult self is here for her, that I will take good care of this little girl whom long ago I named Orphan Annie, and who still, obviously, needs me.

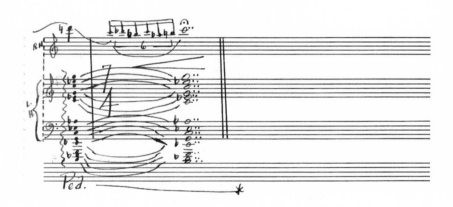

Magical Play

Late November

After Jeff died, I continued our New and Full Moon ceremonies. These rituals helped give me continuity during the immediate aftermath. Their biweekly lunar rhythm also helped to structure my life and attune me to natural cycles, since the shock of his death had catapulted me unanchored into a diaphanous fog.

Our hour-long lunar ceremonies had included the following: To begin, we would smudge ourselves with sage and sweetgrass to cleanse our auras. Then we would invoke the four directions and invite whatever guides wanted to show up. Next came the heart of the ceremony, a short meditation followed by truth telling; here, we took turns speaking our personal truth with the talking stick (often relating insights that came through in meditation) while looking into the other's eyes. Then we would consult with certain symbolic languages, each picking a card from several of the following: Tarot, I Ching, Medicine Cards, Runes, and/or Soul Cards. Finally, we would close the four directions, dismiss our guides and thank them for their presence.

We used to prepare for ceremony by setting up a temporary altar between us, creating a circle from symbolic objects with personal meaning. After Jeff died I continued this part of the tradition, too. In fact, the only part of the ceremony that I couldn't do without him was the talking stick. For this I substituted writing in my journal.

During the first few months post-death, I felt him still present, so much so that only in rare moments did I drop into the sudden bleak awareness of being utterly bereft and alone. Usually I felt completely warmed, loved, enveloped in his aura. So it was natural for me, in preparing for these biweekly ceremonies, to include both his and our objects along with my own on the altar.

After the June memorial, I noticed that, despite a continuing tug towards him, I needed to create the altar with only my own symbols. I would also place a symbol for Jeff—but off in the corner, not in the circle. I was allowing him to look on, but not to be inside. I knew I needed to separate and felt he knew this, too; we were in the process of disentangling our auras, but there were times when I felt him glued to me, and psychically batted him away. He probably encountered the same stickiness from me. All this, of course, occurred on subtle levels.

For the past six weeks I have not done these ceremonies, since I happened to be out of town. But I certainly didn't want to miss the New Moon/Total Solar Eclipse of November 23, due to fall on 1°14 Sagittarius, exactly upon the difficult opposition between Mars and Uranus in my natal chart.

While setting up the altar, as usual I picked objects that symbolized aspects of myself. And, for the first time, I did not include a symbol for Jeff in the corner, looking on. In fact, so much had I separated out that I didn't even notice—until now, when I tell this story—that for the first time there was no ambivalence, no thought that the New Moon ceremony was in any way connected to my relationship with Jeff. I see this as a personal breakthrough, in that part of what had originally attracted me to continue this ceremonial practice after his death was its reminder of our life together.

I smudged, called the four directions and any guides that wanted to come, and went into meditation.

During the meditation I was surprised to note that I sensed Jeff's presence—and not alone, but with a group! The exact experience is hard to describe. It was not as if he had decided to come and brought a few others along with him for the ride, but as if he and the group, he-in-the-group, came in as one entity, working in concert, a group mind. And that in this group he felt very much at home, serene, at peace. I felt both Jeff's kingly Leo presence and his warm Buddha nature. Given what I sensed as his attitude, this was obviously a group of equals, though I had no sense of the others as individuals.

When I came out of meditation I wrote all this down, while feeling sort of foolish, thinking I was probably making it all up. Then I drew an animal from the Medicine Card deck, and got "Beaver." That's when the magic began, and continued into the next day.

Beaver is an animal known for hard work. "Busy as a beaver," we say. As I read through the author's interpretation of this animal, my spine tingled—sure sign, for me, that I am on the scent of something real. As I wrote in my journal, quoting the book: "To accomplish a goal with others involves working with the group mind. Group mind constitutes harmony of the highest order without individual egos getting in the way."

There it was, the phrase "group mind." *I was reading it right after I wrote down the same phrase to document my experience in meditation.*

This synchronicity seemed to open a door; I now felt I knew what had been going on since I had last done ceremony. During those six weeks, I sensed that Jeff had been gone too, working on unfinished ego business. His serenity in the group surprised me, and appeared to be clearly a function of a new self-integration.

In life, Jeff's genius had separated him from others. He wanted to connect, but he also needed to be himself; so if he was fully himself in a group, others were usually intimidated. However, in a group of unique, fully individuated, self-expressive equals, everyone can relax and feel at ease.

I realized that by appearing to me in his full Leo self inside a group of Aquarian equals Jeff had gone beyond me, and was now showing me the way. (Aquarius is the sign opposite Leo in the zodiac. As Leo is self-centered to the exclusion of others, so Aquarians tend to be both individualistic and yet work well in groups. The two signs need each other. Every sign needs to absorb the characteristics of the sign opposite in order to evolve.)

During this eleven-month-long grieving process, I have often found myself looking back at the two of us, viewing and feeling memory tableaux as I circle round them; the view alters slightly as I go, offering subtle new angles of vision, each a thread that continues to weave meaning into a more and more dense and richly hued texture.

Now, with this new Leo/Aquarius insight, for the first time I could see the two of us as having had damaged egos when we met, and that our lack of ease with others had been part of what drew us together!

My awareness then spiraled back further, beyond Jeff. I started to notice for the first time and in great detail that I have had difficulty with every group of which I have been a member starting of course, in childhood. I was the first of eight children, displaced further with the arrival of each new baby, and longing, *desperate*, for solitude.

All my life, except for brief periods of numb, dumb

obedience, I have been a renegade, a rebel—touchy and defensive, often going against the will of the group, needing to prove myself in the group, feeling suffocated, alienated and/or bored with the group, dramatically breaking off from the group, and so on. Of course, everyone has moments of rebellion in groups. But those moments, for me, had extended into seemingly permanent states—poses, if you will, ways of defining myself, of actually carving out my identity in opposition to the will of whatever group I was in. Only now do I realize this means that all these years I have still been in the process of individuating, not yet secure within myself, not comfortable in my own skin.

I really have to laugh when I notice the personal truth of the old adage: "We teach what we have to learn." For my two preoccupations have been astrology and community. I love astrology in part for its capacity to address the full unique nature of a being, and for its ontological assumptions: that all beings are of great and equal value; that if we all operated according to our original natures, our world would be in harmony. I've often told clients, "If you aren't expressing your nature fully, then there is a hole in the universe where you are meant to be." And, further: "Just follow your nature, and Nature takes care of you."

My interest in community dates to a bright winter day when children in our suburban neighborhood, usually polarized into cowboys and Indians or cops and robbers, found ourselves building a snow house in the neighborhood park. For one entire afternoon grace descended. It felt as if we were all embraced within a larger awareness, as kids of all ages organically and calmly cooperated in the various tasks of rolling snowballs big enough for building blocks, deciding on what block went where, lifting them into place, filling in the little holes, deciding where the doors and windows would be. Our strange unity felt like an altered state; it both mystified and delighted me. I never forgot that day.

Nor did I forget my time as one of the teenage dancers in a community musical, *Annie Get Your Gun*. For that six-week period of rehearsals culminating in the excitement of opening night, a group of fifty or so people worked together in harmony towards a common goal. A special feeling enveloped us all; I was keenly aware of this feeling, and it filled me with wonder.

So these two preoccupations, astrology and community, expressed astrologically as Leo's emphasis on self-centered, personal expression and Aquarius's focus on experiments in group cooperation, have been both my passion and my Achilles' heel.

Jeff had exhibited the same Leo/Aquarius neurosis, though I would say that, even taking into consideration his difficult personality, he was more capable of working harmoniously with groups than I. In his work with both the international Trager community and the Jackson Hole Jewish community Jeff felt utterly at home.

I don't have genius as an excuse. So what is my problem with groups? Maybe it has to do with my eldest child status. Is this pattern so hardwired that I've always had to dominate, cowering in groups where I couldn't? Maybe I've unconsciously picked groups in which I could feel either superior or inferior or both, because I have been afraid to actually join forces with equals and fuse into the shared power of a group mind. But if so, then this is a projection, since I have long taught others that the "unintegrated ego" is out of balance—either too big, lording it over others, or too little, feeling inferior—or both. I cringe now to remember how I would smugly admonish Jeff for *his* unbalanced ego.

Clearly I am still working on this, what for me seems to be a lifelong issue.

When Jeff and I got together, we quickly created a universe of two inside the larger one. We depended on each other, and spent a lot of time massaging each other's touchy egos, fending off the outer world.

Since his death I have cut loose from all the groups in which I had participated. This was easy to do, since we had so recently moved far from friends and family. I was also surprised to find myself intensely grateful to be living in a new town where I hardly knew anyone. And more than anything else during this period of mourning, I've had a powerful need to rediscover and center myself in my own life, in conscious solitude, after the rich and complex—and in part, neurotic—duet Jeff and I played out while together.

And now, I realized during this New Moon/Solar Eclipse ceremony, my dear Jeff was showing me the way back into the group. It dawned on me that I am in the process of healing my own ego in solitude, that this healing may eventually magnetize my rightful place in a circle of equals.

As usual, whenever a synchronicity stops me in my tracks and floods me with meaning, the astrology of the situation yields another synchronicity, connecting above to below, to further illumine the situation and place it in a more cosmic context. This symbolic language has long been so much a part of my life that I cannot help but notice planetary correlations during times when I stumble upon a cache of hidden significance.

Usually I don't discuss the astrology of a particular situation to any but astrologers, since its meaning tends to be difficult to convey. But the astrology of the Group Mind/Beaver eureka moment seemed so exacting and precise that it felt like a capstone on what turned out to be the first act of a two-act play.

I am going to make an effort to present the astrology of this particular synchronicity clearly enough so that a layperson can understand it. I hope that it will intrigue you enough so that you too may begin to recognize how the exact timing of the intersecting orbits of two (or more) heavenly bodies does seem to mysteriously reflect and symbolize events in our own personal lives. (In case you're concerned that "astrology is fatalistic," I would say it's true! The planets *do* pull our strings, in the sense that the timing of their movements mirrors the activation of our unconscious tendencies. However, I would also say that when we make a concerted, long-term effort to wake up and take charge of our lives, then we can use the energies of the planets to help us comprehend and even amplify our own conscious evolution.)

My awareness of the uncanny timing of planetary configurations floods me with a feeling of utmost security. I sense myself as the center of a universe that has no circumference, so that every point in it occupies the center. When I feel my awareness spread from my own small life into the stories told by movements of heavenly bodies, I feel showered with blessings from that magnificent cosmic dance—so much so that even my grief eases when I place Jeff, myself, and our connection inside this larger order.

However, should the whole idea of astrology leave you cold, you are welcome to simply skip to the next chapter!

Before I detail the astrological synchronicity of that December solar eclipse and its aftermath, I need to present some background.

Between April 1995 and March 2003, for a full seven years, Uranus—the planet of rebellion, genius, iconoclasm and the ruler of Aquarius, sign of group effort and the group mind—traveled through its home sign, Aquarius. In late February 2003 Uranus crossed over the final, 29th, degree of airy Aquarius to tentatively dip its toe into the early degrees of watery Pisces, before it turned to "go retrograde" and backed up into Aquarius for a final few months—and a final Aquarian lesson.

In late September Uranus moved from 29° to 28° Aquarius, then turned to go forward on November 8, 2003 (also the date some have called the "Harmonic Concordance," a Full Moon/Total Lunar Eclipse integrated within a six-pointed "Star of David" Grand Sextile planetary array). As if to underscore the drama of the upcoming symbolic shift, Uranus remains in the final degree of Aquarius until the final day of 2003. On January 1, 2004 it ushers in a sea-change in the global atmosphere when it enters Pisces for its next seven-year run.

During my New Moon ceremony on November 23, Uranus was at 28°59 Aquarius, within one degree of conjunction to my natal 27° 07 South Node of the Moon. Since the cycle of Uranus is eighty-four years long, this conjunction has never happened before in my life, nor will it again. Each transiting conjunction of a long-cycled "outer planet" (Uranus, Neptune or Pluto) to a natal planet in your chart is a once-in-a-lifetime opportunity.

Events that occur during the first cycle of any planetary energy contain information that you can access for the first time. So you would think I would have been paying particular attention to this one-time-only transit of Uranus to my South Node. But my attention had been diverted to another important transit. (Astrologers reading this will understand why: transit Pluto nears conjunctions with my Ascendant, Sun, Venus and Mercury.)

The South Node, along with the North Node, 180° away, which it opposes, is one pole of what can be called the karmic/dharmic axis. The lunar nodes denote the degrees at which the Moon crossed from the ecliptic north and south on the date of birth. This axis functions as a homing device, or direction finder, to orient us from our past to our future. The South Node feels karmic; it includes old patterns that both serve as a foundation for the future and need to be transformed.

My South Node, in Aquarius, concerns patterns I developed with groups. And given the location of my South Node in the third house of siblings, I deduce that, at least in this life, the pattern began in my original (Aquarian) group of eight brothers and sisters. Our parents wanted to be fair, and they treated all of us equally—to the point where, unfortunately, they found it difficult to recognize and honor the (Leo) specialness of each of their very different children.

The North Node, representing the future, is the dharmic end of this axis, what needs to be integrated to travel one's own unique path. My North Node is in the sign opposite Aquarius, namely Leo, in the ninth house of higher learning and of philosophy, in which field I received a Ph.D. (This philosophical theme is buttressed by my Sun, Ascendant and Mars in philosophical Sagittarius, the natural ruler of the ninth house.) In early adult life this ninth house emphasis on having and teaching my own (Leo) very different philosophy and value system evolved into an estrangement from the prevailing world-view in the department of philosophy at Boston University, and from that of my own family. My philosophical reorientation was in part, I now realize, my way of separating out from the group in order to establish my Leo identity.

I have long paid close attention to this Leo North Node, and have known that for me to continue on my path I must develop in my own way, apart from others. So the relative solitude of these past months has felt both natural and appropriate. Indeed, I was extremely grateful that thanks to Jeff's estate I finally had the opportunity to walk this path of aloneness in ease and comfort, after sixty long years of trying, and generally failing, to both work with and, for economy's sake, live in, groups.

In my natal chart the comet Chiron, at 28° Leo, conjuncts the North Node and opposes the South Node. Chiron symbolizes both one's original wound and the healing of that wound. With Chiron conjunct the North Node, I need to discover what has wounded my Leo ego, and work to heal it so I can follow my unique Leo path.

Jeff's Sun at 28° Leo exactly conjuncted my Leo North Node and Chiron, and formed a harmonious 120° trine with my 27° Sagittarian Sun. So it's no wonder I felt so at home with him; no wonder we naturally supported each other's egos. And we were also both petty tyrants, fearful of each other's dark moods. Especially in the early years we clashed repeatedly and wounded each other's egos. I imagine we both intimidated others more than each other, however. Those rare raging fights got things off our chests and cleared the air.

And now, during this late November New Moon/ Total Solar Eclipse that conjuncted my natal Mars/Uranus opposition, I was seeing the concurrent transit of Uranus to my natal Aquarian South Node as if for the first time. The moment felt truly magical.

Here was the group (Aquarius), and my habitual rebel stance within it (Uranus). And here was Jeff (in a group), present in my New Moon ceremony, shedding new light on that current transit of Uranus transit over my South Node transit. Jeff's presence in a group helped me to understand that I too, no matter how solitary, need and can learn to function effectively as an equal in a group.

This was an astonishing moment: I realized that Jeff and I were still learning from each other, despite him having been dead for nearly one year.

And now for the second act of this magical play.

The day after my ceremony I was to frame one of my watercolor paintings and take it to a gallery to be hung for a new show.

I have been painting for a number of years, sporadically and by and large fearfully, burdened with an old childhood feeling of "no talent." Jeff had championed this part of me, and had on a number of occasions spent lavishly on art supplies. Like a child needing parental approval, I would show him each painting as soon as it was done. He would praise the effort and even, on occasion, praise the piece.

When he died, I avoided my studio. I felt lost in this aspect of my life without him there to help me move through chronic fear.

About a month after Jeff's death I invited a woman over for dinner, and she happened to look into the studio and notice my paintings on the wall. "Oh!" she said, "you should join our co-op and put a painting in our next show. Use *this* painting [she pointed to a self-portrait that I thought ridiculous]. Due in tomorrow! Here's the address." She scribbled it down on a piece of paper.

I was stunned—and, though still doubtful of my talent, thrilled to be asked to join the artists' co-op (another Aquarian group!). I had missed Jeff's feedback and now I was going to get feedback that was even better, because more objective, from the public!

This artists' coop puts on a new show every six weeks, each one theme-based. This motivates me to overcome inertia (fear) and get into the studio.

For the early autumn show, in September, I had added far-away birds to a Wyoming mountain scene painted earlier, to qualify for the theme called "Aviaries." I wasn't happy with the piece as a whole, and ended up framing it with only the center showing, floating in a large mat. Framed, it looked like a miniature. At the gallery, feeling foolish—this was the first time I was actually to offer a painting for sale (I hadn't been able to part with any of the others I had shown)—I gave it a $75 price tag.

When I went to the opening a week later, I noticed the other paintings were mostly in the $300-$400 range.

I only stayed for a few minutes, and very few people were there. But one man did stop before my painting. Braving trepidation, I went up and stood next to him. He asked if the painting was mine and then said, "I like it. You should raise your prices."

You can imagine my thrill in receiving feedback from a stranger.

Now flash forward to November, the day after the New Moon ceremony when Jeff had appeared with a group. I was taking in a painting for the next group show and wanted to retrieve the other one.

I apparently arrived at the wrong hour, because the only person there was a woman working at a desk. Our gallery is also the lobby of a local theater company (another Aquarian group!), for which she said she was a volunteer.

I went to take my "Aviary" painting off the wall, when she looked up and said, "Oh! That is *your* painting?! We just love that painting. All of us just love it!" I was stunned of course and said, jokingly, "Well then, why didn't somebody buy it? It's only $75!" "Because," she replied, "the people who put on these plays make only $10,000 a year."

Another stunned moment. Then, impulsively but strongly, I said, "Well, who would appreciate this painting the most? Who should I give it to?"

It was her turn to be stunned. Recovering, she said with no hesitation, "Candy. Candy is the one. Every day when she comes in here she stands in front of it and says how much she loves that painting." Then, she said, as if she had just remembered, "Oh! Candy is here! Do you want to meet her?"

"Sure."

She was gone for a few minutes, and came back followed by a young, heavyset woman. The woman looked puzzled and somewhat scared. Why would she be summoned to meet a stranger? What had she done?

"I hear you like my painting," I said, by way of introduction. She looked puzzled. The woman who had gone to get her said, "You know, the painting on that wall, the one you love so much." Candy turned back to me, and gushed, "Oh yes, I just love that painting! I love it so much that every day when I come in here I stand in front of it for a few minutes."

"Well," I said, "it's yours."

"What?! Mine?!" She looked completely ill at ease now, utterly out of her element.

"Yes. I'm giving it to you."

"What?! You are?!" The reality began to sink in, and she started to weep.

"Yes. Because I'm told you're the one who loves it the most." By this time I was beginning to feel about my painting as if it were one of my kitties. I want them to feel at home with a kind cat-sitter when I am on the road. I want my kitties to be happy. To me, this painting was now alive, and needed a loving home.

I told her that, and she of course started to pour out

her thank yous, which embarrassed me.

To distract her, I asked her about herself. She is an actress and a singer, "a Leo," she said. And as she said that I could feel her queenly self rise up and shine forth. I asked her when she was born. "August 22." Jeff's birthday.

Jeff's birthday!

Only later did I recognize the playful reverberations of this event with Candy: Jeff, who loved to act in plays, who had been trying to bring his singing voice back during the years before he died, who was overweight due to his love of candy. . . . We had even placed candy on the memorial altar as one of his symbols.

And only now, as I wrap up this chapter, do I realize what, besides the presence of Jeff, connects the two acts of the story. I had been scratching my head, wondering why the two acts felt connected.

I am amazed at how dense I can be when looking at my own "stuff." Of course! The two acts are connected because Leo is about creativity. Jeff, the Leo, had championed my creativity. Chiron there showed the wound ("no talent"), which needed to be healed, and North Node pointed the direction into the unknown future. I was now a self-expressive Leo member of an "artists' cooperative" of Aquarian equals. It's about time I recognize that, get to know the other artists, and enter into artistic dialogue with the larger world.

And what, I ask myself, does the giveaway of my painting, and the incredibly warm feeling that enveloped me when I did that, mean? Can it mean that as Jeff gave away his material goods to me, enabling me to center and ground myself while nurturing my own creativity, so now I am to give of my abundance whenever the moment presents itself as appropriate—and that I give unstintingly, with no thought of reward, just as he did to me? Just as, when he was alive, I admonished him to do with others?

Yes, it must be. For how else could I even begin to express my heart-bursting gratitude during these eleven long months—gratitude for the gift of his presence in my life for those miraculous twelve years; gratitude for the gift of his startlingly beautiful death as the clear climax of a long-unfolding, heartwarming drama; gratitude for the gift of security he lavished on me in dying; gratitude for the healing of my own self-expressive creativity; gratitude, finally, for the continuing gift of his serene, caring, cheerful presence as I peek out now, from beneath the covers of my solitude, to encounter a brand new day.

The Amaryllis Bud

First Anniversary

I had been warned that the holidays would be difficult. Yet to my surprise they were not difficult; indeed Christmas near Boston with my children and grandchildren felt like a loving immersion in a ten-day-long warm bath.

Prior to leaving for Boston, and without realizing its Aquarian import at the time, I had decided to give a party on January 4th, the anniversary of Jeff's death. I wanted to honor both those who knew him in his short time in Bloomington and those who had helped me during my first difficult year as an isolated new widow in a brand new town. These included the postman (who wrote "deceased" on all Jeff's bulk mail so I wouldn't have to) and the law school dean (who forgave Jeff's loan), plus neighbors, my art teacher, my handyman, and others—all invited as Aquarian equals!

So during my visit in Massachusetts I was subliminally preoccupied with the upcoming party, concerned that it go well. I am not a party person, so it felt strange to put on this event, but something in me felt it appropriate. Even so, the task of integrating such a mix of people who did not know each other and barely knew me seemed daunting. Jeff's dad had generously offered to pay for it, so I decided to have the party catered, hoping that good food and service would help create an atmosphere of celebration and honoring.

Meanwhile, in Massachusetts, as "Granny Annie" I read books to insatiably curious three-year-old Kiera, played on the floor with sweet baby Drew, helped my delightful daughter-in-law, Sue, in the kitchen, and hung out at the kitchen table with my two full-hearted sons.

Nights, however, were another matter. (As another new widow with whom I compare notes reported on her holidays: "In the daytime I was fine, even organized a sing-a-long at the piano with my family one evening, but at night? I would climb in bed and wonder what I was doing there. Nothing felt real.") So I was fine and felt loved and loving, but I also felt like an alien. My unconscious used sleep time to continue the mysterious personal overhaul that follows the death of a soulmate.

Take this dream, for instance, one of a series having to do with structural change:

> *I am walking around a very large two- or three-story house, kind of like an old manor. I have just bought it? With Jeff? It has many large rooms, but is in dire need of renovation. I walk onto the large lawn, notice that the white paint on the whole back side of the manor house is peeling badly. It looks decrepit.*

> *I wonder if, instead of renovating, I should raze it and start over.*

An outer world situation then indicated just how ambivalent my current mood. For, when I opened the front door on my return to Bloomington, I noticed that it squeaked. Over the next few days the squeak turned into an ear-curdling screech. I had to laugh. What a perfect metaphor for my reluctance to open my door and admit people in! And of course, I fretted as to how I would direct them to the back door and avoid the screech. A dear neighbor, an older man, offered to fix it. First he oiled, then greased, the hinges. The door still screeched. He concluded that it must have been hung wrong. But there was no time to rehang it before the party, to be held Sunday evening from 5:00 to 7:00 P.M.

On Saturday it started to rain, and by Sunday the water cascaded in sheets. Radio and television announced road closures due to flooding, and rivulets began to creep across my basement floor. I worried if any of the thirty-five people invited would come. The caterer was to arrive at 4:00 P.M., but due to his restaurant basement flooding, he was an hour late. Amazingly, he and the guests all came within minutes of each other, so I just had to tell the first people to go to the back door and all the others followed.

This initial crush in inclement weather was probably key to the party's success. Guests took food and utensils from the caterers' hands as they ran back and forth through muck from the truck to the back door. By the time everybody was inside and dried off, our flooded basements had bonded us; food and wine flowed freely.

The party ended way past the stated hour and closed with a toast to Jeff, while we gazed at his benevolent beaming face hanging high on the living room wall of family photos.

Afterwards I walked around the empty house in a daze, amazed that the party was actually over, and that it had exceeded expectations.

Then, suddenly, I felt the urge to do ceremony. My personal ceremony. To close this first and primary year of grief in my own way, privately.

As usual, I lit a candle and called in the four directions, plus any guides that might want to come. I was now quite comfortable with doing ceremony alone, and for many months had not included personal objects of his on the little altar created for the occasion. His presence, likewise, strong at first, had faded—until he arrived with his group during my November ceremony.

So you can imagine my surprise when I noticed during my meditation that again Jeff's spirit was present! And again he seemed to be with others. There he was, serene and cheerful, still delighted to have rejoined his soul group, operating as a group mind.

Then I experienced a most peculiar sensation: the feeling of many hands on my head, covering my head like a cap, in benediction. I got the impression that I was being told, "You did a good job." With what? I wondered—the party? This past year? My life? Life with Jeff? I didn't know.

Once I came out of meditation and started to write down the experience in my journal, I began to doubt myself. I must have been making it all up, I thought, and wrote that down too.

Within days of this event, I received a dream:

I am trying to follow in the giant footsteps of a shaman. Must complete a task that is impossible, until I allow others to help me.

Meanwhile, however, I was still working with grief, still needing my aloneness. On New Year's Eve, only days before the party, I had gone to the movie *Cold Mountain*, and on the way home surprised myself when the keening— so prevalent during the first few months after he died, but rarer since then—that had germinated within me during the entire month of December finally took me over. There I was, driving home at night with headlights glaring into my teary eyes as I erupted into the usual howling, images of Nicole Kidman and her doomed lover swirling into images of Jeff and me.

From my journal:

"Very strange. It's like we were all one being, or that the four of us swirled into each other and the intense emotions of love and grief and loss were moving through all of us. Felt the usual protection, enveloped in an aura of love, while undergoing this."

The next night, this dream:

I am talking with Jeff, who is in a different body. Or not in a body, but there is a body there, representing him. It's a male body, sort of wooden. There seems to be another spirit there too, who came with him. I am asking Jeff questions, and he is doing his best to answer. Since he is moving objects around, I ask how is this possible? He says offhandedly, like the answer is obvious, that they use energy to move them around. Another question, maybe my last one, is about whether or not he wishes he were in a body (since I sense it would be more convenient, if he wants to work within the material dimension), and his answer seems to be ambivalent. He enjoys his freedom, but he would like to have the ease of working in this material world. I also sense that he would like to be in a body so that we could feel each other, hold each other.

An addendum to this dream: During the month of January, on several occasions I was puzzled to discover toenail clippings on the living room floor (I used to bug Jeff about clipping his nails on the couch and leaving them on the floor). I sensed that he leaves them for me to find.

January proved much more difficult than December. It was not the holidays but the anniversary of his death that got to me. I was starting Year Two without him, and felt sluggish, bogged down, my sadness and grief mirrored by a persistent low-level lung infection and by continued grey skies, gloom and rain after the four inches received the weekend of his party.

(By the way, the day after the party I had called my handyman, who had been unable to attend the party, to come reinstall the door. He took one look at it, pushed up hard on the frame above the door several times, and . . . no screech! Thanks to the party, the door to my life with others could now open and close without squeaking.)

In mid-January, in an effort to jumpstart my stalled life, I decided to dedicate Saturday and Sunday afternoons to art, at least two hours each day. I began by drawing the amaryllis plant that a friend had brought as a gift the night of the party.

My journal records how that decision then segued into the unexpected:

"For the past six days I have spent two or more hours a day painting the opening of an amaryllis bud. An amazing experience. The flower grows faster at its leading end, where matter differentiates into more and more delicacy. So I have to keep up with its growth. And seem to be getting better at painting it as it grows. It caught me. One day I was just painting the bud, and the next day I found myself painting it again. Then again, and again."

But, I discovered, once the plant fully flowered I could not paint it. Though I tried several times, my attempts felt dull and lifeless.

So, looking as usual at events in the outer world as mirroring inner conditions, I realize that I am still a bud, that while I can now enjoy a bud's first growth spurts, my full flowering lies in the future, and cannot be anticipated or rushed.

Meanwhile, my artistic efforts were affirmed in a dream of being at a chaotic construction site for a huge new school:

> *I am in one of the large four-story square pods of which it was composed, and in the middle signing up for classes. It seems to be the art department, with lots of different kinds and sizes of notebooks, paper, etc., and I must take one of each for my own.*

The exciting sense of new construction by night, however, was still stymied by lung and sinus congestion, and the continuing sluggish feeling of no energy and no motivation, no reason to go on. In my journal: "So, on balance, it feels like I am still in the transition between the old life and the new. But that the new has more energy in it. Something about me and Jeff is keeping me stymied at some level?"

On January 17th, I dream that I am driving the car I owned when we lived in Jackson Hole, Wyoming, up a mountain valley. The mountain reminds me of Snow King, behind the town of Jackson.

> *As I go up the tracks get narrower and narrower. I end up next to the top on extremely narrow tracks, and turn the wheels to the right to keep the car from going down. Even then, I have a sense that I may have difficulty backing up the car.*
> *I get out, and go out on the well-used trail.*

*I am anxious about the trip down and, when I
survey the situation, notice that the track that the
back tires are on (they are turned to the right, at
right angles to straight ahead) is so narrow that the
two ends of the tires stick out over nothingness.
Now I am extremely concerned that I will not turn
the wheels properly to align them with the narrow
track, which will mean that I will slip off the track
rather than being able to back up. I realize I need
someone to help me see the back end of the car
while I am trying to back it up. And actually, the
situation looks impossible whether or not someone
helps me.*

Again the need for help, for not thinking I have to
be independent all the time, is present. But beyond that, the
dream puzzled and unnerved me.

Three days later, from my journal:

"I think I begin to understand that dream. It has
to do with 'coming back to earth' after the otherworldly
experiences of the past year. How do I get back down? I'm
afraid of falling down. And afraid I can't do it without
help. Or can't do it at all. The reference to my old car and
our old place may have to do with the fact that these fears
are those of the old me."

Then came the dream that still fuels me, and
perhaps will for many, many years. A very powerful dream,
of which only fragments remain.

*Of being with Jeff; though he is invisible, his spirit
is very strong, and fills the same space that his body
did. Telepathically he encourages me to hold him,
to hold on, just like I always did when he was alive,
using now, his spirit as a battery. In the holding on*

he feels as solid and substantial as when he was in body.

Next scene: I am walking slowly, haltingly, groping my way, like into a void. Either I am blind or it is so dark and foggy that I can see nothing of what lies ahead. But it doesn't matter. I am filled with his presence, loved and protected as I move into the future.

This dream felt so strong that I sensed it as a new foundation for my life. I tried to describe the special status of this dream in my journal: "The dream resided at the bottom of a well, at the center of a dream within a dream, a frame within a frame; or better, at the inmost core of a beating heart."

Meanwhile, rain had been followed by unusual cold. I didn't dare expose my still-congested lungs to the cold for fear of making the situation worse. So although my low-level physical illness was gradually clearing, since I wasn't energized by my usual long walks both the feeling of being stuck inside the house and the lack of desire for life persisted.

One day at the end of January I decided I had to take a step into the future, despite my depression. That even though my lungs weren't quite healthy, I still needed to get outside, and do something that was so different from my usual routine that it would shock me into another mood. I decided to go snowshoeing in the nearby state park, telling myself that even if I only did it for ten minutes it would be enough; at least I would have done that one new thing. I loaded the snowshoes in the car and drove out to Brown County. When I turned into the entrance to the park I noticed that it cost four dollars per car for the day; I almost turned back, figuring it would hardly be worth it if I only stayed ten minutes.

I decided to push on through that little obstacle too, and plopped down the four bucks.

Amazingly enough, I snowshoed for forty-five minutes in the trees of those gently rolling hills. Though of course I missed Jeff, as he used to love to snowshoe too. I regretted having given away his snowshoes only a few days after he died. (Widows are warned about this tendency to immediately just give things away. The snowshoes were my one impulsive move in that direction. After that I became more circumspect, recognizing the danger of not truly knowing my own mind in the immediate shocking aftermath.)

The sun slanted through bare branches onto stiff old pockmarked snow as I chugged along, alone but okay, growing more and more aware of the light and shadow of that silent day, my legs powerful from my daily morning tai chi routine, memories of snowshoeing and skiing in wild Wyoming cheering me on. I was clearing old fuzzy cobwebs out of my skull. I was that amaryllis bud—thirsty, finally given water to grow.

I came home tired from my little adventure but strangely energized. Amazingly, my lungs actually felt better! Immediately, I decided to: (1) paint my study, and (2) buy and install the L-shaped desk I have wanted all my life. What better way to inaugurate my new year, my new life, my new dedication to the writing life?

My young cat-and-house-sitter agreed to be hired for these tasks. We had fun. Painting the room took a few hours, installing and putting together the desk of my dreams took most of a day.

I sit here writing this at my beautiful new desk, in a room newly painted in a warm color called "Wheatfields."

The back and forth between old and new continues. I haven't put the drawers in the desk yet, or put together the hutch that goes on top of it, and my right hand still bears traces of a burst blister from screwing in all those screws. But I have survived. And though I am blindfolded, and still groping, Jeff lives deep inside me. I am filled with his presence, loved and protected as I move into an unknown future.

* Arpeggiate these chords slowly

appena sensibile

Jeffrey Joll   10 October 1964

Strands of the Goddess's Hair

Have you ever wondered, while standing by the ocean, about the ebb and flow of the tide? How is it that we can be so aware of the colors of the swell, the traces of salt?

Last August, at Gerstle Cove in Northern California, I became aware of one possible learning from this. I had walked down to a protected tidal pool where the summer before I had received a blessing from the waters, to sit and watch starfish and crabs and mussels climb over stones in their drive . . . where?

Contemplating the slow movements of these creatures, I looked further out onto the rocks that protect the cove, saw a seal edge slowly into the water and became aware of the way the waves were broken up by those rocks. And in that awareness of the connections between life in the tidal pool, the sea and the land, I saw the Goddess in her sea form, with the reflection of sunlight through the top layers of the sea Her eyes, and the tracings of salt left behind by the tide became Her hair, streaming over the land/seascape in benediction.

—Jeffrey Joel, 1990

"Just remember, Ann. We're making it all up!"

—*Jeffrey Joel (on many occasions)*

Appendix

*A*n Astrological Commentary

On the Life and Death of my Husband, Jeffrey Joel

May 25

> *"Jeff was rather like a flower, blooming ever so briefly with exquisite blossoming, and most of the time growing in hiding where only those who had eyes to see, might."* —*Tasha Halpert*

Introduction

I first encountered Jeff Joel at a conference in San Francisco on "Cycles and Symbols," where I was a presenter and Jeff sneered that he was "slumming." The next day he showed me his astrological birth chart, which left me gasping. I had been a student of astrology for nearly two decades, and had never seen a chart so difficult.

I met Jeff on July 26, 1990, the very day when Pluto turned to go into direct motion after six months retrograde. Even then I was intrigued by the Plutonian symbolism, and later considered this day a perfect one to initiate our relationship, since it promised a life together of continuous transformation.

As a double Sagittarian, I am intrigued by challenges, accustomed to risk, and can be a fool who acts on impulse. So of course I invited him, only one week later, to leave his seventeen-year tenure as an editor for *Mathematical Reviews* in Ann Arbor, Michigan, and come dwell with me in a tiny yurt in a tiny village in the valley of the Grand Tetons.

I didn't realize it then, but my invitation activated both of the only two harmonious aspects in his birth chart. First, his natal exact sextile (60°) between loving Venus and unpredictable Uranus was stirred up by the chemistry between us: those planets were in near-exact opposition (180°) and trine (120°) with my Sagittarian Sun. Furthermore, his other harmonious aspect, also an exact sextile, between natal Mars and the Ascendant, was at that time opposed and squared (90°) by transit Uranus, making him unusually restless.

However, with seven planets in fixed signs Jeff was a very fixed fellow, and I imagine that were it not for one other deep background aspect currently playing upon him, he would have waited until the Uranian energies settled back down and then lapsed into his old life with the usual complaints about how boring it was.

But the ground had already been plowed internally for a massive uprooting from his old tired world. Pushing him over the edge into utterly unknown territory was transit Pluto, planet of death and rebirth, which, for about a year, had been bearing down on his natal Moon/Jupiter in Scorpio. This aspect began with an operation to remove twelve inches of his colon; it also brewed up a hornet's nest of long suppressed emotional needs.

Little did I know when I tossed off that invitation, as if it might be "fun" to have this unusual man join me for awhile, that I had thrown down the gauntlet: my challenge was exactly what he was unconsciously seeking—a life-changing, precedent-shattering event.

The sleeping giant was aroused. Six weeks later he gave up everything for yurt life in Wyoming with a woman he barely knew.

"Oh my God! What did I do?"—gasped my Venus/Mercury in Capricorn, stiff with fear.

He assumed our arrangement temporary, a way to spend his sabbatical year. I don't know how I knew, but I knew that he would never go back. One year later, he resigned his position.

Our relationship did not start as romance, but as combat. Rather than having stars in our eyes, we plunged deep into the Shadow. My Sagittarius was righteous and dogmatic, wanting to change and improve him; my Capricorn wanted to tame the beast. All attempts were met with a baleful Scorpionic glare, forcing me to see my manipulative meddling in that reflective mirror.

Of course I wanted him to change, because he was so rude, selfish, and inconsiderate! And I had invited him to live with me?! But our fiery Suns were closely trine, and his Sun was conjunct both my North Node and Chiron. Looking back, I would say that we were partnered from the beginning; we didn't need the initial romance to attract each other; simply, our karma had come due. And once begun, there was no way out. I didn't even consider it.

Jeff entered my life just as transit Jupiter returned to the degree it was located at my birth, 23° Cancer; he died a little over twelve years later, when Jupiter returned yet again to that natal place. One Jupiter cycle. One cycle of opportunity this Sagittarian wasn't about to miss. Furthermore, not only was Jeff in an unusual Uranian phase; so was I. He came to live with me on the very day transit Uranus turned to go direct exactly upon my 5° natal Venus in Capricorn.

As an astrologer, I knew he was incredibly "fixed." Whatever movement he made would probably be glacial in pace, scouring the rock of his foundation, but, in the short run, hardly discernable. My skill in reading birth chart energy patterns did prove to be crucial in navigating those early months and years. Had I not been able to see through the thick emotional scar tissue to the magnificence of his essential nature, I would not have been able to even begin to connect with this initially shy, proud, powerfully irascible man.

During our first year together, he was sunk in the depression and lack of self-worth he had dragged with him from Michigan to Wyoming. Though my personality thought me an idiot for having invited the monster in, apparently my soul knew not to let his miasmic sludge-like appearance stop me from being with him and gradually gaining his trust. Bit by bit we opened to each other; looking back, I can see how, by continuously rubbing against each other's rough edges, we slowly surrendered to our larger beings.

At first, though, we were honorable opponents, engaged in dharmic combat between two immensely stubborn personalities, each determined to prevail. With seven planets fixed, he was much stronger than I in his capacity to remain stuck, and to resist appreciating my company. But I also persevered, thanks in no small part to my stubborn Taurus Moon, which grounded both inner guidance and the usual native optimism. I knew with every fiber of my being that his birth chart promised the light of his original Leo being, shining in a cave, below all the armoring.

Looking back on our relationship now, I honor that long difficult dance for its gifts of patience, endurance and especially, compassion. I can usually catch myself now when I turn dogmatic and preachy, so much did his mirroring force me to surrender that old persona.

Birth Chart

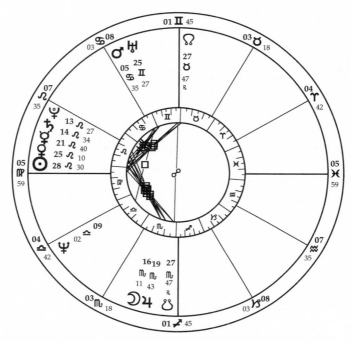

Jeffrey Scott Joel was born on August 22, 1947 at 6:55 A.M. EDT, in New York City, with five planets in fixed, fiery Leo: Sun, Mercury, Venus, Saturn and Pluto. His nature was to be highly creative, generous and big-hearted, dramatically self-expressive. Moreover, his Sun was located in the 29th degree of Leo, exactly conjunct the great star Regulus: he seemed to have arrived on earth as an old, old soul, an ancient King, born with a silver spoon in his mouth and a natural sense of entitlement—which however, had been destroyed somewhere in the deep past. Jeff reminded me of the Grail Legend's Fisher King, whose kingdom lay in ruins.

For there were, in this life, three qualifiers that tended to spoil the Leo magnificence unless he focused on being utterly conscious and aware of how he used his energies.

First, all his Leo planets were in the karmic twelfth house of the chart, hidden away, nearly impossible to consciously access. Indeed, many times over the years, sensing turbulence beneath the stoic mask, I would ask, "What's going on, Jeff?" and he would respond, forlorn and resigned, "I don't know."

Second, two of his Leo planets were difficult: Saturn and Pluto, and in tight conjunction. This conjunction is generational, a signature of those born during the "Saturn/Pluto in Leo" years, 1946–1948. These years ushered in both strong generational leaders (e.g. Steven Spielberg, Hillary and Bill Clinton) and leaders with a conscious or unconscious tendency towards fascism; these years also birthed a rash of severe casualties (like burned out hippies and alcoholic Vietnam War vets). It may be that many Saturn/Pluto in Leo people were, in recent past lives, either persecutors or persecuted in the concentration camps of World War II. In any case, they seem to carry memories of power and the abuse of power, and I sense that Jeff, for one, feared (Saturn) using his power (Pluto) lest he hurt people.

And third, all Jeff's Leo energies except the Sun were in a tense, 90° "square" aspect to a tight conjunction between Moon and Jupiter in Scorpio. Scorpio is a fixed water sign, desiring to enter deeply into relationship; yet, for Scorpio, any perceived betrayal or disloyalty from the one to whom he dares bare his soul is deeply hurtful and deserves instant, lifelong animosity. This combination of sensitivity and attachment to pain can lead a profoundly disappointed Scorpio to become both secretive and paranoid.

The combination of these three qualifiers meant that Jeff, despite being gifted with five planets in Leo, did indeed spend most of his life hidden from view, nursing his wounds, both paranoid and afraid of his own power, and unable to consciously access his own creative energies.

The great heart originally promised by Leo was matched by a profoundly curious and omnivorous brain. (And like many in a society that values brain over heart, for a great part of his life Jeff focused on learning and attempted to deny feeling.) His Scorpio planets were in Gemini's third house, and he voraciously absorbed any subject that stimulated him, reading and speaking in many languages, delving deeply into science, history, literature and the occult.

Jeff's South Node of the Moon was also in Scorpio's third house, so this scholarly focus was natural to him, something he had brought over from the past. However, his Taurus North Node of the Moon called him to gain perspective by grounding in his physical body and in the earth, something that our primitive yurt life demanded: every day, all winter long, it was his job to chop wood and carry water. Furthermore, those lunar nodes enclosed all his planets and were in close square to his Sun: with every major decision he had a karmic choice: go for the future, or remain stuck in the past.

In coming to Wyoming Jeff left his academic home to discover a home that called him to his senses. He attuned to the Moon shining through the yurt dome as it crossed, waxing and waning, through the brilliant night sky. He absorbed the wind's many voices, and the telltale sounds of rain, sleet and snow through the yurt's thin translucent skin, as well as footfalls of wild animals passing to drink from the tiny creek nearby, the calls and swooshing of raven and hawk wings . . . .

Though his decision to move to a tiny yurt in Wild Wyoming surprised many people, as a member of the Uranus in Gemini generation (1942-1949) Jeff was not only attuned to science, mathematics and new technologies, but also to any number of alternative, radical, innovative ideas. Moreover, Uranus, in the tenth house of his path, was the leader—the engine—of the train of all his other planets (going clockwise). He was known in the world as a Princeton/MIT mathematician, capable of teaching an introductory graduate level course in any branch of mathematics. Even after leaving *Mathematical Reviews*, every year he translated and reviewed books and hundreds of mathematical articles from all over the world.

His Leo planets in the Piscean twelfth house held a natural resonance with music, which he discovered at an early age. He composed music, studied piano and many wind instruments, accompanied professional soloists in concerts, played in orchestras, sang in choirs, and continually listened to both world music and especially the great western classical music, singing along to tragic romantic dramas of Wagner and others while reading their orchestral scores.

From childhood on, this twelfth house of dreams and the imagination was Jeff's real home; he spent much time there, in reverie, seemingly far from Earth. Through the few cryptic remarks he made to me about his life in the dreamtime, I can report that he seemed to be reaching for the harmonic laws of the universe governing visual and spoken languages, music and mathematics; that through an attunement with these laws he seemed to be attempting to divine the laws of creation. I like to think that eventually he even included human feelings in his appreciation for the whole.

As he grew older this twelfth house Piscean coloration of his Leo planets, combined with his third house Scorpio's profound love of study and his discriminating Virgo Ascendant, led Jeff to explore and be trained in alternative healing modalities. During his final twenty years he made himself available as a healer using Trager bodywork, Alchemical Hypnotherapy, and shamanic ceremonies; however, his essential Piscean shyness and lack of ease in the social world meant that only those few who could feel him beneath the mask asked to receive what he had to offer.

The midpoints of his Leo/Scorpio planets all converged on or near his Neptune in Libra, a generational signature active for those born between 1942 and 1957. For Jeff, since Neptune was in the second house of self-worth, the value he assigned to himself depended on his making a crucial decision: to follow his own spiritual guidance and, if possible, to enter into an idealistic, spiritual relationship.

Solitude was natural for him: all his planets were on the left-hand side of the chart, making him self-sufficient. But his evolutionary development called for the Other, as well as for using his tremendous twelfth house Leo energies in Piscean service to others. This capacity for selfless service was also shown through his Mars in Cancer, on the cusp of the eleventh house. He mingled easily in groups of people with common interests and he focused his great nurturing energies on a number of alternative communities, midwifing their birth pangs and supporting their early foundational years.

When I met Jeff I intuitively sensed that his main task in life was to evolve into a fully human being. His intelligence and his power were so vast he stuck out like an alien. He told me he sensed he was planted here on Earth for some important reason, but was having great difficulty in finding his path and felt both unrecognized and underappreciated. So when he rose to the challenge of entering relationship with me, he also, so to speak, met his oracle: throughout our time together, I would say to him, "Open your heart, Jeff. Open your heart. Give those glorious Leo energies to anyone who asks. Give selflessly, generously, without thought or hope of recognition for what you do."

In other words, fully utilize that twelfth house Leo through selfless service; integrate those Leo/Scorpio energies by continuously crucifying (Scorpio) the ego (Leo) in the fires of compassion (Pisces/twelfth house).

Now, after Jeff's death, I stand in awe at what seems to be his soul's exquisitely precise fulfillment of the unique laws of his unusually difficult birthchart. He came, he saw, and he conquered: himself. He grew gradually into the magnificence that was his destiny and surrendered ego to love, radiating compassion into the world around him. I am so grateful to have been allowed to witness many of his remarkable deaths and rebirths along the way. And I am astonished and delighted that we, two members of the often delusional Neptune in Libra generation, did actually succeed in creating a union based in the spirit and responding to the spirit's call. Indeed, we saved each other.

Especially in the very end did Jeffrey reveal his true nature.

Death Chart

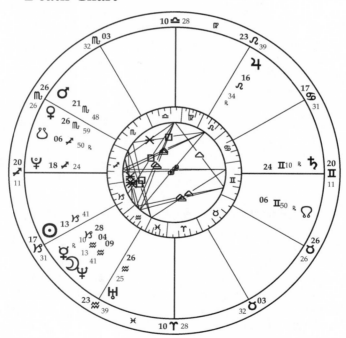

Though I did set up Jeff's death chart on the day he died, my eyes kept blurring when I tried to interpret it. So I put it away. Finally, months later, though still emotionally distraught by the idea of looking at the death chart of my beloved husband, I got it out again and attempted to discern the story it wanted to tell me. I am so glad I did, as it seems to me that the time he chose to die threw what I see as the meaning and purpose of his life into high relief. The planetary synchronicities are so remarkable that once again I am brought face to face with the shining stars and their loving embrace of our tiny world.

The following commentary is, of course, based on hindsight. Though I point to what seems to have been a mysterious plan at work during the final months of Jeff's life, there is no way I could have predicted his death beforehand. I assume the soul can use any number of scenarios to exit from this world, and only point here to the wonderful way his own deliverance took place. For me, Jeff's death seems deliberate, as if his soul composed a beautiful choral piece with many voices, all of which converged in the end into one glorious shimmering chord.

Jeff died at home in Bloomington, Indiana, early on the morning of January 4, 2003. I estimate time of death at about 6:30 A.M. I had cuddled with him in his bed at around 4:30 A.M. and found him sweating; he said he felt cold. I was alarmed, but he said, in a reassuring tone, that he was "fine." I then went back to my bed. At 8:30 A.M., when I arose, I looked in on him and noticed he did not seem to be breathing. As if in a dream, in shock, I came in the room to see the great domed head grey-blue, the eyes half open. His neck was still warm, though his limbs were already cold.

That afternoon I ran a death chart for 6:30 A.M. and put it away. When I finally did focus on this chart I was not surprised to discover that it placed the transiting Midheaven exactly on his natal Neptune. The transiting Pluto/Saturn opposition, in effect since August, 2000, was also significant, since it was at that moment very near the transiting Ascendant/Descendant axis (the East/West horizon).

Many astrologers agree that Neptune and/or Jupiter are the two planets usually activated at the time of death. That these two most "spiritual" planets in the solar system guide us during our most crucial earthly initiation may help us realize that, far from being a terrible, frightening event, death of the body surrenders the soul to the cosmos.

The two axes, the Midheaven/Immum Coeli and the Ascendant/Descendant, measure the earth's daily rotation. The earth revolves on its 360° axis once every twenty-four hours, or approximately one degree every four minutes. Thus any planet transiting over any of the four points described by these two axes covers that point for only four minutes. Thus these four points set up the exact timing for events.

These two axes—one vertical, the other horizontal—are also the foundational structure for the person's interaction with the world. Midheaven and Immum Coeli at the top and bottom of the chart symbolize our vertical path in life: we plant our feet on the ground so that we may reach for the stars. The Ascendant/Descendant axis on the horizon symbolizes our east/west relationships with others: horizontal, meant to be equal. These two axes and their four points, called the "angles," are the windows that link the person to what surrounds him.

I have not done many death charts, but those for which I do have precise times all have at least one planet on one of these four angles. I doubt I am mistaken in my assumption that his soul took that precise window of opportunity, during the four minutes when three planets were on or near angles, to exit the body.

(Further anecdotal evidence for the angles as precise timers of our last breath comes from my friend Claudia whose mother tried to go out one day and failed, despite a great struggle; twenty-four hours later, at the same exact hour, she did manage to let go.)

For Jeffrey, Neptune (and, to a lesser extent, Pluto and Saturn) as the precise trigger on the rapidly moving angles of the moment for the soul's release was the end point of what I imagine as a much longer process. I see this process for Jeffrey as a space/time gyre that spiraled in from January 2002 to a certain precise moment on January 4, 2003 when his soul shed its mortal remains and expanded into the larger universe.

Of course there is no absolute way of deciding when a process, occurring in an open system, begins. As the philosopher Ludwig Wittgenstein once said, "It's hard to go back to the beginning, and not go further back." However, reflecting on Jeff's death now, I recognize his climactic journey as a year-long preparation for the enactment of his final earth-bound initiation. And I cannot help but see this process, so exquisitely complex and integrated, as divinely orchestrated.

This synchronization included transit activation on natal planetary positions of background planets, then middleground planets, then foreground planets, and finally the two axes mentioned above, with the rapidly-moving Midheaven aligning exactly with Jeff's natal Neptune as his soul released from body.

And, as we shall see, just as his natal Neptune was activated at the final endpoint of the gyre, so, one year earlier, transit Neptune defined the widest round of the gyre's spiraling origins.

The deep background atmosphere of what I feel was this ancient soul's year-long preparation for return to source was set up by transits of two of the slow-moving outer planets, Neptune and Uranus. The middle ground was occupied by transits of Saturn and Jupiter, moving less slowly than the outer planets but more slowly than the inner planets. The finalization of the process—the pinpointing of his final days and then his final moment—was set first by transits of two of the short-cycled inner planets, Mars and Venus, and then by the quickly rotating Midheaven crossing over his natal Neptune. In all, seven of the ten planets were involved in the orchestration that crescendoed to glorious finale.

Thus did I feel privileged to witness what Tasha called Jeff's "exquisite blossoming" "ever so briefly" before his great light burst from the spent corpus.

That was a summary; here are some details:

The mood of the entire year leading up to his death was set by transit Neptune, which since late January, 2002 had been crisscrossing 9° Aquarius in an exact harmonious trine with his 9° natal Neptune. Jeff's spiritual nature, always so prominent given the Piscean coloration of his natal Leo planets and natal Neptune as midpoint of his Leo/Scorpio stress, was at ease with itself, opening into the vastness.

In March, 2002 transit Uranus began to crisscross in opposition to his natal Sun and trine his natal Uranus. He was excited, and in a fashion very unlike his usual torporous self, eager for rapid transformational life-change: he looked forward to moving out of Jackson to become a newly minted law student.

All three aspects made by Neptune and Uranus were once-in-a-lifetime, long-lasting transits. The synchronization of these three notes sounding all at once for such a long time made this a year like no other; big changes were not only possible but invited.

In the middle ground were Saturn and Jupiter, both also activating natal planets.

Transit Saturn reached the conjunction of his natal Uranus for only the second time in his life in August, 2002. This transit remained in effect until May, 2003. August was the month we moved to Bloomington, Indiana, in preparation for his matriculation at Indiana University Law School. He was even more excited (transit Saturn now joined transit Uranus in aspecting his natal Uranus) and the long-awaited plan (Saturn) was finally taking effect (Saturn).

In October, approximately one month after starting law school, transit Jupiter in Leo began to move over his natal Leo planets, beginning with Saturn and Pluto at 12°. Expansive Jupiter went up to 18° and then turned to go backwards, not to go into direct motion again until April 2003. Its turning point, in mid-November at 18°, was the midpoint between Jeff's Saturn/Pluto and his Mercury. Remember, Jeff was in a expanded mood during these months, very friendly, open, and talkative, generous with time and energy to all with whom he came into contact. (Indeed, members of his law school class were stunned when I told them that, up until his first (and only) semester in law school, he had been an introverted, more or less reclusive person.)

From the day he died, I have mentioned repeatedly to others that Jeff's open-heartedness came into full flowering during the final two weeks of his life, when, during Christmas vacation, he visited me and my grandchildren in Massachusetts (where I was making an extended visit), and on his way back to Bloomington told his father, for the very first time, that he loved him.

Only now do I notice the astrological signifiers for these final two weeks: transit Venus and Mars, both in Scorpio, came into contact with his natal Moon/Jupiter conjunction in Scorpio. Transit Jupiter in Leo squared transit Mars/Venus, and all three were stimulating those natal Leo/Scorpio squares. His intense love, always so hidden and yet palpable to me and others close to him, warmed everyone with whom he was in contact. That old Scorpio poker-face no longer prevented his great Leo heart, enhanced by transit Jupiter, from openly shining. Indeed, when I opened the front door of my son's home in Massachusetts to find Jeff unexpectedly there, two hours early, I was momentarily stunned by how large and expansive his face was, how it shone with radiance (I had not seen him for two months). My sons commented to me that day on the apparent transfiguration in his countenance. Then, to our surprise, he immediately bonded with my two-year-old granddaughter, another Leo, and they basked for two days in relaxed mutual adoration.

Jeff was no longer hiding. His luminous essential nature was on continuous unselfconscious display. And what I had suspected all along seemed to have been correct: his heart was even larger than that massive brain.

After Christmas, I drove with him to visit his father in New Jersey for two days. At the conclusion of this visit, Jeff took me to the bus for the trip to rejoin my children. This event would be unremarkable except for a moment of extreme poignancy, so intense that I am surprised to realize that I only allowed the memory of it to surface a few days ago. It is this: he has just put me on the bus; I am sitting there, looking out the window at him; he gazes at me with such tenderness and longing, such a sense of finality and stoicism. As if he will never see me again.

After seeing me off, Jeff drove to be with his father for one last lunch. It was then that he told his father that he loved him.

I did see my dear husband again however, four days later, when I flew to be by his side on January 2 after a phone call in which he told me he was having chest pain and was going into the emergency room. This pain came on January 1, 2003, the exact day when transit Mars completed its conjunction with his Jupiter/Moon. When I walked into the hospital on January 2 he had just undergone an angioplasty, and was, amazingly enough, sitting up and feeling fine, just as expanded and loving as he had been for the two weeks prior to this invasive procedure. (This is rare for heart patients, who typically come out of heart procedures depressed and anxious.) I picked him up the next day, and on the way home he told me that he was feeling good, not at all the way he felt after his first heart attack five years ago.

That night we enjoyed a joyous, loving reunion, unusually relaxed and caring. (It was a such a thrilling shock, the next day, to recognize the evening before as our finale. That we were gifted with such a loving goodbye!) We retired to our separate rooms, and I went to him at 4:30 in the morning, wanting to hold him. That's when I discovered he was sweating, and cold. But he assured me he was fine, so I returned to my own bed.

I assume that synchronous with his last breath, the Earth had rotated to the exact moment which would place the quickly-moving Midheaven on his natal Neptune and transit Pluto/Saturn near the transiting Ascendant/Descendant. It appears that he went out as a child of the spirit, having completed what I imagine to be his lifework: opening that vast heart into compassion for all of creation.

I wince to notice that, due to both genetics and eating patterns (he was somewhat overweight), the physical heart was not capable of carrying the great current that had begun to course through it. Such an exquisite, poignant paradox! For as his emotional and spiritual heart opened, so did his physical heart fail him.

I can stay there, with that terrible knowing, or I can move into equanimity, and understand that his life purpose was achieved. There was no more need to be here. He had realized his fully human nature and could be about his work on the other side.

His ecstasy as he released from body was palpable to me, and for several months following his death I participated in an indescribable sense of joy and freedom, simultaneous with my initial shock and grief. I attribute this easy spillover from him to me across the dimensions to the fact that for both of us, our natal Sun/Jupiter midpoints were conjunct his natal Neptune. As our relationship in life was spiritual in nature, so was our parting equally blessed.